Dream House

Eight Steps To The Peace And Joy You Deserve

Dr. Judi Bowman

LoveLight International Press

LuvPress@aol.com

Also by Judi Bowman

Rebuilding the Wall:
21st Century Inspirational and Womanist Poetry

Showers of Bliss:
Your Portable Paradise of Inspiration and Hope

DREAM HOUSE:
Eight Steps To The Peace And Joy You Deserve

Copyright © 2000 Judi Bowman

Published by: LoveLight International Press
          LuvPress@aol.com

PUBLISHER'S NOTE:
The names, places, and incidents contained in this work, have been changed to
protect the privacy of the informants. Any resemblance to actual persons, living or
dead, events, or locales is entirely coincidental. This work is designed for spiritual
enlightenment purposes only.

For book signings and direction on booking Dr. Judi Bowman:
e-Mail: judiprays@aol.com

Programs include: "The Total Package": Holistic Development Series, Spiritual
Development Retreats, and Fitness and Nutrition Coaching

For ordering information please contact Bookmasters at:
Sales: 800-537-6727
Internet: http://www.bookmasters.com and http://www.atlasbooks.com
e-Mail: info@bookmaster.com

All Scripture quotations, unless otherwise indicated, are taken from the HOLY
BIBLE, NEW INTERNATIONAL VERSION® NIV. Copyright © 1973, 1978.
1984 by International Bible Society. Used by permission of Zondervan Publishing
House. All rights reserved.

Cover Design: Ad Graphics, Inc.
Front Cover Hair: Jacqui Compton
Front Photograph: Andrea Waller Photography
Back Photographs: Studio 9E and Oneal's Studios
Manufactured in the United States of America.

Bowman, Judi.
Dream House: Eight Steps to the Peace and Joy You Deserve/ Judi Bowman.
ISBN 0-9677019-1-0

DEDICATION

*This book is written
for this generation. May you walk in the peace,
joy, power, and light of God.*

*And for my son,
Ollie "Tiger" Monroe Bowman Howie,
whose laughter, love, and prayers
brought me closer to my own Divinity and more in
touch with the real of me.*

CONTENTS

* * * * *

ACKNOWLEDGMENTS

Not all women, in fact, very few have had the blessed fortune to live out the desires of their hearts. I thank God for his graciousness to me. Many of us live in environments where living in peace and joy is simply a dream. It is my hope that this publication will bring the dream of living in peace and joy to fruition to all who read it and spend time in the silence. I believe that God has given me the time, resources, and gifts to come to you in truth, and as Mother Shirley Chisholm says, "unbought and unbossed."

I am especially grateful for the affirmation and guidance given me by the Holy Spirit, whose imprint is on every page.

THERE are too many people who have directly or indirectly contributed to this work to express my appreciation to them individually. Jo Kadlecek deserves the credit for having encouraged me to stick with the conceptual framework and the very heart of the subject matter in this book. She spent hours with me on the phone and in my hotel room in New York listening, asking questions, and encouraging me to be myself ("Judi Truth").

My agent, Greg Johnson, at Alive Communications has supplied the encouragement I needed to be real to the *real* and not to the *role*. Dan Rich, Liz Heaney, and Erin Healey at Waterbrook Press spent countless hours reviewing my outlines and have maintained my faith in the worth of this kind of undertaking.

My thanks to the many informants and their families is perhaps best expressed by the publication of their portraits.

Sara Lawrence Lightfoot, Preston Williams, Connie Williams, Joe Maxwell, Barbara Neufeld, Jay Heubert, Helmet Koester, Elisabeth Schulsser Fiorenza, and the late Paul Ylvisaker, my professors and advisors while in graduate school at Harvard, gave me the tools to be a social scientist and ethnographer turned writer. They taught me how to analyze social settings, integrate Biblical principles, and give life to message of hope God has graced me with. I appreciate their faith in me.

Thanks is given to Michelle Gilliam, my personal manager, for being frank and firm, which compensated for the friendly and fair elements of my personality.

There are many preachers and authors who have inspired this work, and I quote nuggets which they have poured into my life.

I wish to thank Sonya Banks, Deborah Sanchez, Kim Felder Johnson, Malverna Streater, Joy Hill, Jeanne Darden, Marvin Stewart, Robert Scott Jones, Luvenia King McLean, Tobi Cole, Elaine Flake, Janette Bowen, Sharon Ingram-Redcross, Reneatha Macklin, Karen Page, Cathy Krinick, Carleton Ashby, Mom Dorothy Ingram, Gary S. Nachman, Wesley Rice, Jennifer Smith, Monica Jenkins, Cynthia Burse, Carole Copeland Thomas, Cyne Alexander, Carol Hovey, Lyn Hovey, Patrice Calloway, Shirley Chisholm, Clementine Freeman, Stacy Whiting, Hattie Allston,

Savinah Hughes, Ophelia Howe, Vanessa Rice, Odessia Hawkins, Tara Hux, and Jaynelle Oehler for their good wishes, support, and sufficient prayer covering.

I express deep appreciation to my mentor, William R. Harvey for his encouragement over the years and for appointing me author-in-residence at Hampton University as a platform for touching this generation for Christ.

I am grateful to my teacher and coach, Michael Kelly, for teaching me to celebrate each season of my life and teaching me what it really means to ascend.

I am thankful for my pastors Bishop David Copeland and Claudette Anderson Copeland for their inspiration, example, and covering.

Last but not least I wish to thank my family for loving me, praying for me and allowing me to break out of molds, design my dream home, and literally live in it.

PART

1

The Design Phase

"Seek peace and pursue it"
(Psalm 34:14)

I Want To Live There!

*A Blueprint for Living in the
Peace and Joy I Deserve*

L ife is a celebration. Let's tap into it. You can imagine a life of peace and abundant joy just as you can imagine what your dream house, dream kitchen, dream closet looks like. In this book, there are two types of women: the princesses and the pressed. The princesses know God, and live in peace and joy; they live in "dream houses." A princess is anchored in the power and presence of almighty God, so whether she is asleep or awake, she is in touch with her Divinity and in touch with the peace and joy which are part of her very being. Her reality is dream-like because, to her it is a way of life. To others it seems "fake," "phony" or impossible because, "the light shines in the darkness and the darkness has not understood it" (John 1:5).

Her antithesis is the pressed woman. The pressed know God, but do not know peace or joy. They aim to design and live a dream house, but instead get caught in the press of being overwhelmed by their lives and paralyzed by their own personal problems. I want to take you on a tour of a dream house (the inner chambers of our hearts) so that we may get things in check, and ultimately live as princesses, heirs of the Most High God, so that God can use us to touch this generation and fulfill His plans in the earth.

Through the use of a dream home as an analogy, this book provides us with a practical remedy for creating and maintaining peaceful, joyful lives in the midst of everyday challenges. *Dream House* relates to the motives, attitudes, aspirations and goals we have as women who are devoted to God and determined to live in peace and joy.

I wrote *Dream House* to help us examine the spiritual, emotional, and physical blueprints which we live by, in the privacy of our own homes (hearts), in order to nurture peaceful, joyful living. Why in our homes? Women love to nest. Whether spending the night in a hotel room, guest house, new home, shelter, trailer, or a car, women have to have their nests straight. It is home, for however long; and home is the heart of a woman. Therefore, the principles for peaceful, joyful living in this book address the very heart of women by leading us into spiritual wholeness, which is something pressed women only dream about.

The eight steps and principles of *Dream House* reflect the particular areas of the home as an analogy for self ex-amination. Just as there are several different rooms of a home, so too, are there different "rooms" in our lives and hearts.

Each chapter, then, enters the analogy of the room and uses it to examine the different areas of life. From the front door (our image) to the kitchen (our sources of nour-ishment) to the bedroom (our place of intimacy), I prescribe eight practical principles for creating a healthy life overall. I have collected data from hundreds of interviews with women and combine their stories and my story with Biblical and contemporary examples and portraits. Consequently, this book offers easy to read, step by step advice for determining the quality of our emotional and spiritual lives, and for redesigning it accordingly.

By the conclusion of this book, you will have formed a picture of what your "dream house" (joyful, peaceful life) could look like: uncluttered, focused, seeking purpose in life, moving toward your goals, enjoying and celebrating each moment, and above all, not simply existing and being torn apart by every trial which comes your way. The woman who lives in peace and joy, the princess, moves through the storms of life with endurance. The race is not given to the strong or the swift, but to the one who learns from adversity and keeps on going! When a woman lives in peace and joy, she is doing meaningful things she enjoys and enjoys the things she must do. Hers is a non-violent, focused, life of love, celebration and calm. *Dream House* will help you to become a princess or a more disciplined princess in a world where many women are pressed.

By the time you finish *Dream House*, you will have a thorough understanding of the journey you personally need to take in order to design or redesign your "dream home." You will also have specific principles which you may choose to implement in order to begin (or continue) your dream life—life of peace and joy. By remembering the analogy of the dream house with all of its rooms, you will also be able to take specific, practical steps to apply what you have learned as well as confessions which give power to those applications. You will learn that faith, God-consciousness, and your perspective have more to do with creating a dream home than do your circumstances, other people's opinions, or anything else outside of yourself, your heart (your home).

AN INVITATION TO DESIGN YOUR DREAM HOUSE

This book could have been called *Eight Steps to a Perfect Life*, or *Disciplines for a Life that Everyone Longs For* or even *The Peace and Joy Book*. It could have been titled something other than *Dream House: Eight Steps to the Joy and Peace You Deserve*, but that is what I call it for three reasons.

First, princesses live in castles, dream houses. When you were a girl, did you dream of a being a princess in a castle? Me either girl, but it sounds dreamlike. I never dreamt of a castle, but I was once a guest at the Spencer House in England, the childhood home of the late Princess Diana of Wales. I even came close to being a princess, four times—once as homecoming queen at Phoebus High School; and then as Miss Freshman and Miss National Honor Society both at Hampton University; and a final time as Myron Howie's bride in my Priscilla of Boston gown. I have many sweet memories and so do you, but let us put aside this archetypal notion of princesses so that we may go beyond the superficial, skin deep issues and get to the real things that dreams are made of.

You may be a princess who lives in a 3.5 million dollar mansion in Scottsdale, Arizona or one who calls her dream house a section in a homeless shelter in Roxbury, Massachusetts. The beauty of it all is that the dream house concept is all a part of our perception because each of us has different needs, temperaments, destinies, and stations in life, but we can all dream; and we call all live in peace and joy.

Second, the house concept is important to us as living creatures. We need shelter and we are programmed to nest and set up home wherever we find ourselves. Home is familiar, home is comfortable; and in this book, it is the paradigm for teaching us how to receive, cultivate and walk in the fruits of peace and joy.

Through the use of a house as an analogy, in this book, I teach about creating and maintaining a peaceful, joyful space in the midst of life's challenges and everyday events. By using eight areas of a house as symbols we walk through each area to determine in what ways and by what means we may be able to evolve and line up with Biblical and practical truths and ultimately live in peace and joy. These eight areas represent different parts of our lives and they help to create:

- peace and joy with God

- peace and joy with ourselves

- peace and joy with others

- peace and joy with this world

Third, this book is about finding the peace and joy you *deserve*. Yes, you deserve it. No matter what anyone has told you—God loves you; and you deserve peace and joy because it is a gift from Him. You do not deserve to live in hell. Hell is *not* a place for princesses.

*"This is hell. There must be a heaven,
because this life is hell."*

Darla, a forty-nine year old married, white mother of three grown children and two adolescents. She works twelve to sixteen hours per day at a Las Vegas, Nevada department store loading and unloading stock.

"This is hell. We live in hell."

Brenda, a twenty-four year old, single, black mother of a four-year old, HIV-positive son who lives in a Boston housing project with her HIV-positive mother, sister, and grandfather. (She said this as we drove up to her apartment after our interview. One of the dumpsters was literally on fire.)

"My life is hell. I have to leave this place"
(current place of employment).

Ann, a thirty-seven year old, white, single, international portfolio manager in New York who works at the same firm as her ex-beau, who is now engaged to a twenty-five year old secretary who also works at the firm.

I don't know about you, but all of my life, I have longed for sweet peace. I have longed to fulfill my purpose; I have longed to live in the abundance and joy which God promises His children. Although I am still evolving, I am there; and I want to take you there, too.

Now, this book is not designed for us to condemn ourselves. No one is one hundred percent, as Mom Dorothy puts it. Princesses understand that there is a difference between condemnation and conviction. God does not condemn us; but the Holy Spirit convicts us because of God's love for us. We are all evolving. No one has kept all ten of them, because we are sinful by nature, but that does not give us license to live in the press. If we were judged based on the historical factors of our lives, then we would have no hope for the future and no blood to cover our sins. Our lives are more than what others see. Every princess realizes that she is in need of self examination.

How Do We Examine Ourselves In Order To Be In A Position To Walk In Peace And Joy And Live In Dream Homes?

Examining ourselves can be compared to grooming ourselves. When I look in the mirror, I say, "I need to shape up my brows" or "my brows look really decent today, thank you, Father." Some women need professional treatment for their hair like chemicals and colors. Others just need to wash it and go. So it is with self examination; it is a very personal experience. We need to become naked and not ashamed if we are to live in peace and joy. Being naked means looking at ourselves without the make up, without the padded or push-up bras, and without the clothes and jewelry with which we often adorn ourselves. It means being who we really are, not who others perceive us to be. Come and walk with me. Let's get real and examine ourselves.

Questions And Statements To Consider:

1. What hinders my close fellowship with God? (God is a jealous God. If a habit, relationship, obsession or aspiration is more important to you than God, ask Him to remove it.)

2. What have I learned from my life? (Do you have a quick temper? Are you quick to judge others? Do you live in pity or self condemnation?) Ask God to remove these things from your life and don't beat yourself up while He is helping you to redesign and rearrange.

3. Am I seeking *God's perfect will* in all situations?

4. What are my motives? (Some people want a gift, object or relationship to "show off" or to look good to other people. God wants our motives to be pure and in line with His divine will)

5. What is my purpose?

6. Am I comparing myself to someone else or am I listening to God?

7. Am I sincere?

8. Do I have unresolved anger issues?

9. Did I stop to pray today? Do I pray and meditate enough or at all?

10. Do I listen to God?

11. Once I hear from God, do I obey?

CHECKING MY ATTITUDES AND ATTRIBUTES

When examining ourselves we need to realize that the world does not revolve around us, our needs, our problems, our world view. We can't expect folks to rally around us because they have not traveled the road we travel. Rather, God wants us to trust Him to order all things in his Word, find favor, and dispatch his angels to guide us in all we do, think, and say.

Princesses are called to strive for humility, modesty, self valuation, honesty, patience, love, forgiveness, simplicity, trust, generosity, promptness, straightforwardness, positive thinking, clean thinking and to look for the good.

Pressed women operate in self pity, self justification, trashy thinking, insincerity, procrastination, laziness, envy, jealousy, resentment, false pride, hate, impatience, dishonesty, self condemnation, self importance (narcissistic entitlement), and vulgar thinking.

As a princess, I can see, hope, imagine, and dream. Come on Paul. What did Paul tell the church at Ephesus? "[God] will do exceedingly above all I can ask or imagine (Ephesians 3: 19, 20). God will do exceedingly, abundantly above all we could ever hope for or dream about. I don't know about you, but I hope for the best, dream for the best, expect the best, refuse to accept anything less than the best, because I serve a God who is the best and who never changes. So, come on sister friends, and dream with me.

"The joy of the Lord is your strength"
(Nehemiah 8:10)

CHAPTER TWO

Nice House! Anybody Home?

A Blueprint for Examining My Motives and Character

Principle: In order to live in peace and joy, I must connect with God, and be clear on my motives for designing and projecting my personal image. I must not let others' opinions of me hinder God's plan for my life.

Confession: I bring God glory because I am more concerned about pleasing Him than I am about living up to others' expectations of me, winning friends and impressing people. My image reflects my true character. They both bring glory to God and show His love in the earth.

This chapter deals with what unlocks our doors or what motivates us to do and think the way we do. For some it is money, power, or praise, for some it is family, God, or citizenship. What type of character do you have? What is really behind that front door? What kind of image are you working on? We are going to spend some time here, sister friends, because once our motives and character are in check, we are well on our way to dreamland— authentic lives of peace and joy.

What Is Image?

Image is what people think we are. God is not concerned about that. He wants us to represent Jesus and have good reputations, but he does not judge us based on what others think of us.

Image is also what we think of ourselves. If we feel worthless, weak, and tired, then the devil has a foothold in causing us to condemn ourselves, causing us to be ineffective in the plans God has for us.

Why Is Self-image Important In The Discussion Of Living As A Princess In A Dream House?

If a woman does not have peace, she will drive in the dark with her head lights turned off, following her husband to work and wherever else he goes. If a woman is pressed, she will be more concerned about the automobile her daughter drives and the home she lives in than her daughter's spiritual and emotional wholeness. The pressed woman will drive herself crazy wondering what people think of her. She will go crazy trying to figure out who was doing what, when and with whom. She will worry whether people think her dress is cheap or too short.

But when a woman has her self-image in check she is not relying on what other people do or say to give her peace and abiding joy. Her peace comes from Jesus, who came to give life, "and give it more abundantly." Her life is abundant because she is not self-centered, but God-centered. She does not think, me, me, me, me. She asks, "what are my marching orders, God?" She listens to God and hears Him speak. A woman at peace has her image in perspective and knows that she is a royal, stable, long-lived, durable, incorruptible, virtuous heir of God. In fact, she is a princess.

LOOKING BEYOND MY FRONT DOOR

Looking beyond the front door, on the other side of the image which others see, we need to line our character up with what God says in order to live in peace.

Her name is Tiffany. Actually Tiffany is not her real name, but I will tell her story to help us understand more fully why we have to individually look to God and listen to Him for our ideas and motives about the image we create and often cling to.

Tiffany was the shining star of her city, from being crowned Miss California to being a Rhodes scholar. She seemed to have it all together. As her best friend Nora often told her, "you did all of the 'right' things. You waited until you were married to get pregnant. You waited until you earned at least one degree before marrying." She was beautiful on the inside and outside. She was a genuinely interested volunteer who had engaged in mission projects since her teenage years. She just loved to help people. A nutritionally conscious fitness queen, she was thin, her hair was healthy, her skin was flawless, and her wardrobe was the icing on her cake.

Tiffany married, Forrest, a professional football player who, because of his salary and love for her, was able to build her the house of her dreams, buy her a fancy automobile, take her on five-star trips around the world, and allow her the luxury of rearing her three young children at home. Tiffany had diamonds and pearls, had traveled the world, and her family Christmas portraits resembled the model portraits in the Olan Mills Photography studios.

Since Tiffany had always been organized, aggressive, and very successful, it was natural for her to do *all* of the house-keeping, serve as Forrest's social secretary, nurture and discipline their three children, maintain the fantastic land-scape, bring in the fire wood, decorate for holidays, attend parent-teacher meetings, attend meetings of the football wives, corresponded and send gifts to family members, and work with service people whom she felt often tried to take advantage of her "easy going" husband, who was loving but paid very little attention to details.

It was also natural for her to care for her husband when, after the birth of their third child, he became psychotic. His inattention to details increased and his behavior often became erratic. Tiffany, the missionary at heart, who was devoted to her husband, their vows, and their family, would go so far as run down the street with her then six month old daughter in her arms after her husband who would panic and run, half naked eating the leaves off of trees and ducking into neighbors' yards. She helped him with his work out during off-season and even made excuses for and cleaned up behind his inconsistencies. Forrest was not him-self, but Tiffany began to see a pattern, which had been going on for years. He had been sick since their first date, but because of her devotion to him and dreams for them, she believed God for his healing and kept taking care of him. When he was admitted to mental hospitals, she would make arrangements to take her children to see him daily—she so much wanted him to feel loved and part of the family in spite of his mental illness.

Tiffany tried to ignore scary things he said during some of his episodes. Once Forrest was in a rage and said that he was sexually attracted to his oldest daughter. He told Tiffany, her father, his mother and his sister. When she brought it up in a counseling session, Forrest said, "you betrayed my trust." Tiffany loved Forrest, but at the same time wanted to protect their children. She did not know if what Forrest was saying was a prophecy, the devil speaking through him, or his true feelings.

From the outside (the front door), it looked like the perfect family, but only Tiffany knew what was going on inside. They had a perfect image, but inside it was if she were riding a roller coaster. Her devotion to God and her family superseded what others might think of her, so she pressed on in therapy with Forrest while continuing to rear the children, maintain the household and keep Forrest's "secrets."

She felt it necessary to keep the secret of his illness because people don't accept mental illness the way they do physical illness. Had Forrest been diabetic or paralyzed, it would have been "acceptable," but because his illness was mental it was different *for him*. The second time Forrest was hospitalized, he asked for Tiffany's father, Tyler. Since the football team had released him and bought out his contract, Tyler told Tiffany to sell their home and move the family to Oakland, California so he could help her with the children and Forrest. When she put the house up for sale she had concerns because, as in the past, people noticed Forrest's lethargy and tried to take advantage of them. Tiffany confided in their attorney, Les, about Forrest's illness because so many people think that since Forrest is wealthy that he knows "everything." Forrest blew his stack when Tiffany told him she confided in Les. From that point on, in honor of her husband's wishes, she continued to keep his secret. She told people he retired from football because of stress.

She had one baby still nursing on her breast, nonetheless, she packed the family and all of the belongings, with Forrest's help, bought a house in Oakland, unpacked everything and set up house alone, found a Christian psychiatrist and the nearest pharmacy, quickly enrolled the older two children in school, became active in church, found the health food and natural stores, and tried to start life all over.

It was very different now. Forrest no longer had the game of football which he loved. He was no longer "the star" on the field and at charity functions. He was home. He loved spending time with the children and did a great job of finding creative child-friendly outings, but things were different now. Tiffany was becoming so tired after taking care of Forrest and the children for nearly 15 years. She felt as if she were taking better care of the whole world than she was of herself. Now she had the added pressure of being back in Oakland where she was, as her mother called her, "the shining star of the town." She could not go to the local convenience store, market or office supply store without grooming herself and three children to the hilt because it would never fail that someone would tap her on the shoulder and ask, "Aren't you Tiffany Taylor?" or "I taught you in high school, and you and your art have been such an inspiration to us." When she and her family would go to church, She would rise at about 4 AM, spend time with God alone, get dressed, cook breakfast, put dinner in the crock pot, press clothes, polish shoes, take Forrest his medication and breakfast on a tray in his trophy room (where he slept on the floor since shortly after their move to Oakland), dress the younger two children, brush teeth, pass out offerings, drive the children to Sunday School, teach Sunday School; and usually Forest would meet them just before church service was about to begin. They would sit, the four of them, well dressed, well fed, as her dad would often say, looking like "the All-American family." Tiffany's stomach was almost always tied in knots because she was sleep deprived, emotionally neglected (because Forrest preferred to work on his computer, play video football games, and rest), and always in a rush.

Tiffany loved Forrest, loved helping him and loved the times they laughed, prayed, traveled, and talked, but soon after they moved to Oakland, they had an argument while she was holding their baby. Forrest, frustrated, prepared to spit in her face and then kicked her twice with great force. She grabbed the baby's diaper bag, her purse, took the oldest two children to her a friend's house and went to the police department. When she left, Forrest said, "I am sorry, baby." He quietly asked, "Do you forgive me?" "Yes" she whispered through her tears, and left.

When she got to the police department, the officer who took the report wanted to have a police car pick Forrest up and charge him with battery. Tiffany refused saying, "I just need to talk to someone, but he is a good man, please do not arrest him. I also just need to have his psychiatrist check his blood to be sure his medicine is at a therapeutic level." The officer called the battered women's hotline for Tiffany. "Sick?" The lady from the hotline asked her. She then went on, "I don't care if he is drunk, on medication, or half dead; if he abused you once, he will do it again."

Forrest had always neglected Tiffany for football, but he loved her, encouraged her, prayed for and with her. "He would never be violent with me again," she thought. Later that week, she even destroyed the police report she had filed. She never tucked money away for a "rainy day" because she was not building a case against the man she loved, she simply wanted peace in her home and joy in her life.

For the next year, Tiffany says, it was business a usual. She continued to do all of the cooking, cleaning, "taxing," nursing, bill paying, word dropping, scheduling; and in her flesh, she was tired. Tired of people taking advantage of Forrest when they assumed that he was "normal" and wealthy in a town where people did not have a lot of disposable income. She became tired of being so busy doing things that were outside of her "calling" that she had little time to do what she thought God had called her to do. She is a painter; and many of her paints had dried in the past year. She loved painting uplifting landscapes and delivering them to nursing homes, women's prisons, family and friends. She had not painted one complete canvass since she had moved back to Oakland. Tiffany was tired. Tired of everyone *thinking* they were the perfect family. Tired of her father, who invited them to Oakland, to help them, but soon after the move, he became so involved in church and volunteer work that he rarely came to their house. She said she felt as if she and her family were drowning; her father offered to save them. He threw them a life preserver, but never pulled it in. They were simply floating. She was tired of her mother, who loved to run down her list of accomplishments, never missing a magazine she had been featured in, but who never once called to ask, "How are you doing?" Tiffany was at peace with her parents because she knows that people can only give what they have. Her parents and Forrest, can only give what they had to give. *She had to look within for peace.* She accepted that. But she was still tired.

One day became a turning point for Tiffany. After mowing the lawn, cleaning the house, dressing the children, and getting directions, they headed for a reception in honor of her father and his volunteer work with the United Way. Tiffany gave Forrest the directions and the invitation and he didn't look at them, rather, he shoved them in his pocket and said quickly, "I know the way." After riding for nearly an hour on what was to be a twenty minute journey, Tiffany asked Forrest if they were lost. Instead of saying something to hurt Forrest's feelings, which would not help anyway, Tiffany remained silent thinking, "I guess I was supposed to drive, too—I thought I could catch my breath for a minute."

When they arrived at the reception, Forrest signed a few autographs and then started to wander around. Tiffany found the reception hall and her father, and took the children inside. Concerned about Forrest after about forty minutes, Tiffany went to look for him. She says she felt mad and sad and said very little at the reception. When they returned to the house, the older children went for a bike ride with their cousins, and Tiffany put the baby down for a nap. She then went to the door of Forrest's trophy room and knocked. This was a rare moment when they could talk outside of the children's ear shot. Forrest did not answer the door, so Tiffany knocked louder saying, "we need to talk." She felt helpless, neglected and tired. She knocked louder. "We need to talk Forrest. Our children do not understand when you shut yourself off from us. I don't understand!" "Please talk to me....Are you trying to ruin my life?" "I have given you everything and you shut me off." "I don't want our children to turn out like you...." She went on yelling from her head and not from her heart. She was mad at Forrest's illness; and like a freezer, she began to defrost with brutal rage directed toward him.

Forrest came racing out of the room beating Tiffany as if he were tackling a quarterback. She says he threw her on the floor, choked her nearly to death, put his knee and fist in her face and left bruises on her face, neck and arms. After the beating, Tiffany ran to the nursery to check on their toddler who asked, "what was all of that noise?" She held him and they both went to sleep. That night when their son prayed, he said, "Lord, if you give me a wife I am not going to push her." Tiffany knew that in spite of what her parents, his parents, their siblings, his former coach and teammates, the people in her town thought, she had to ask God what to do.

She and Forrest talked. He was not remorseful *this* time. His attitude was, "you kept yelling at me, what choice did I have other than to beat you and shut you up?" Tiffany cried and pleaded, "I love you, but if you are permanently mentally disabled and I am dead (from you choking or beating me), who will care for these beautiful children whom we prayed for?" "They have plenty of people who love them," Forrest replied.

Tiffany told her two close friends and father of the beating. When she went to church several members asked her close friends, "Does Tiffany's husband beat her?" Despite the makeup and big-brim hat, she looked battered. Her cousin's husband said, "it looks like someone hit Tiff in the face." Shortly after the beating, Forrest never apologized; rather he engaged his wife in helping him reallocate some of their assets so that they would have more monthly income. All of the bills were being paid each month since they had been together, but that still did not give her peace. She was deeply in love with God, and knew that she had made a vow before God, to Forrest and did not know what to do.

She had to listen to God because everyone else had their own opinion. All they saw was her image, when Tiffany saw her life and the great plans God has for it. One therapist told her, "since your husband neglects you, just get a f—k buddy." One of their pastor friends told her, "if you leave him, you will ruin his reputation." The battered women's support people told her, "if he hit you once, he will hit you again, and it will get worse." Forrest's mom said, "I always knew Forrest was a little different." When she told Forrest that she loved him, but for their safety and peace they needed to separate and get counseling, he took it as all out rejection thinking she wanted a divorce. He went into a rage, "if you are divorced, who will invite you to art shows?" "If you leave me, people who want to buy your paintings will not know how to contact you." Forrest thought of every reason why they should not separate, but Tiffany had to listen to God who told her that he loves her too much to see her sad and beaten of course. She also did not want her young son to learn to become a batterer. Forrest hurt her, but since he is limited due to his mental illness, she understood. She forgives him. But her parents, the ones who had given her life, hurt her deeply with the way they clung to their image in spite of her safety, peace of mind, and well-being. She says she forgives them, too.

"You say he beat you, but I did not see it" said Tiffany's father, one of Forrest's biggest fans. He went on, "everyone in this city knows me. You *and* Forrest are *my* children, and this all makes me look bad." Her mother chimed in, "you are the shining star of this town, you have been in magazines and newspapers all over this town and you are invited to art shows all over the world, if all of this (Forrest's illness, the fact that Forrest is a batterer, the fact that you don't live the image people think you live) comes out, your reputation will be ruined. Her mother continued, "Forrest set you up nicely. He gave you everything. You have nothing!" In spite of all of this Tiffany knew that she had a loving heavenly Father who could and would supply all of her needs.

Tiffany could have continued to live in the false image people had of them, or she could trust God and live in peace and joy.

She and her children have been living alone for ten months now. Aside from the money the children get from Social Security because of Forrest's disability, neither he nor any other family member has given them any financial support. When their air conditioner needed to be repaired, Tiffany called and asked for his help, Forrest replied, "I don't ask you to pay my bills at my condo." If he needed the help, and Tiffany was able, she would help, but she held her peace. God had provided for her for the past 42 years; and God was faithful, whether Forrest was or not.

Tiffany's mother, who greatly influences her father, once said, "I have never *seen* Forrest be anything but loving to you and the children." She was dealing with illusions not reality. "Of course, Forrest is not going to beat me up or neglect in front of my mother," Tiffany said to me.

Shortly after the separation, Forrest took the most valuable marital possessions, his trophies, and framed jerseys. It did not bother Tiffany, but she needed an attorney to help her. However, she did not have the money to retain a good lawyer. Her father, Tyler, helped with part of the retainer, but had no more money or interest in assisting her, it seemed. Tyler and Flora, her mother, were upset because she separated from Forrest. Tyler's best friend from church, Duke, had been helping the family with odd jobs prior to the separation.

After the separation, Duke, Tyler, and another man from their church repaired the motion detectors on Tiffany's house. Tiffany and Duke talked that day. When he came later that week to fix the back yard light, Tiffany had been crying because Forrest kept calling yelling at her, bill collectors called daily, and she still did not have the money to engage an attorney. Duke, who was very compassionate, and had been named "Man of the Year" by his fraternity. Her father often told her, "Duke is the best man in the world. You will never meet a better man." Duke told Tiffany, "I will help you." And asked, "When do you need the money?"

Since Duke was her dad's best friend, Tiffany wanted to share with him. "Mr. Duke said he would help me with my legal fees and help the children and me during this season. I know he is your friend and I don't want to disrespect you in any way" she explained to her father. "Well maybe God put him in your life for a reason. You come from a poor family, but we'll pay him back," her father said.

After that time, Duke fixed the roof, shingles, picnic table, dog house, curtain rod, and helped with hauling wood and blowing the leaves. He encouraged Tiffany, like a father, but since he was married, and since he was old enough to be her grandfather, the relationship was never physical. He was her angel and protector.

Tiffany wanted to republish a series of art prints as her ministry and to help with her income, which dropped from $7,000 per month to around $700 after the separation. Mr. Sinclair, who was a custodian at her high school, often gave Tiffany food since, because of her car and the children's trust funds (which were in her husband's name) she could not qualify for public assistance. Mr. Sinclair offered to refinance his home to help her with the prints, but she did not feel comfortable with him because once when she went to the bathroom, he knocked on the door and asked, "can I look?" "Just let me look," he pleaded. Tiffany told him point blank, "These prints are a ministry. They will bless people. You can get sex anywhere, this is not about sex. " "I am not a 'trick' she told him." After that, she never called Mr. Sinclair back. "If God wants me to republish my art work, He will make a way." This reminds me of a poem I wrote titled, "To Women Under Me." You want to hear it? Well, here it is:

I wish to tell the story
To women under me.
I hope that they will listen
And remember this someday.

Do the right thing, Sister.
Whether they're watching or not.
It's not about the getting.
It's about using what you've got.

Put God first; He will supply,
All of your needs each day.
Stay on your knees and always remember
To pray, pray, pray.

No need to trick or steal or lie,
If you're set up to be bought,
They'll buy you 'til you die

You're worth more than a suit or a trip to France,
Don't put your treasures there,
See yourself as a Kingdom woman—
Anointed, awesome, and rare!

(from *Rebuilding the Wall*, 1994)

So Tiffany did not spend anymore time with Mr. Sinclair once she discerned his motives. A similar situation occurred when she and her cousin, Tabitha, were working at the house. An old friend, Sean, came to help them sand some areas on the patio stairs. When Tiffany went upstairs, Sean slapped her lightly on the bottom. She turned and said, "Look, if you are helping me because you know I need help, that is a blessing, but if you are helping me because you want to be with me, you need to leave right now." Sean quietly said, "well I poured three driveways today, and I am kind of tired" and he left. Period. Part of Tiffany's peace had to do with having a clean conscience regardless of what people thought about her or her image.

Duke offered to get a loan for Tiffany's artwork and saw it as an investment, so they faxed a list of the price to republish the artwork along with two of Mr. Duke's bills to his credit union. Later, since Mr. Duke's wife objected to his support of Tiffany's inspirational collection, they never sent the money and prints to the publisher. But he continued to come over, haul wood, and help Tiffany. Once, when her children were at school, Tiffany locked herself out of the house while tending to the dogs. She wiggled the sliding, glass door and got back in. "If I can get back in, anyone else can," she thought. So Mr. Duke borrowed some tools from his job and put a pin in the metal door for safety. He came by to get his ladder and tools, but since Tiffany was not home he left a note saying that he needed to come by the next morning on his way to work to get in the house and get his tools to take back to work. Mr. Duke usually went to work at 4:00 am. Since Tiffany had been getting up around 2:00 am to pray and paint and sing and have quiet time, it was no problem for Mr. Duke to come by and get the tools. At about 4:15 am Mr. Duke came to her home. They talked for a while and he got his tools. Soon after that, Mrs. Duke rang the doorbell and began taking photographs. Tiffany was not sure, but said she had suspected that Mr. Duke must have done something in their 50 year marriage to make her distrust him. Tiffany later found that Mrs. Duke had been following her husband to the house, and had even found Forrest and told him, "I am going to have that bitch's children taken from her."

When Forrest brought the children home that next day after an afternoon outing he shouted at Tiffany, "you slut, I am going to nail you to the cross!" He left saying, "have your friend Mr. Duke give me a call." Once the two talked, Forrest shouted to the top of his voice, "that is my mother fu—wife, and my mother fu—house, and you are disrespecting my mother fu—children." "I was just helping your family" Mr. Duke said as he tried to slip a word in. "If something needs to be done over there, you call me first!" Forest shouted. When she did call Forest to help have the heat pump repaired, he replied again, "I don't ask you to help me pay *my* bills."

Tiffany had an art show at an area school that next Saturday and Mrs. Duke, who had probably seen an advertisement, stormed through the auditorium three times so Tiffany could see her. Tiffany was still at peace, because her hands were clean.

Later her aunt called her and said, "I need to come and talk to you—in person." After her children were in bed, her Aunt Lily came and said, "I believe that you and Mr. Duke are not having a relationship, but there are a lot of rumors that you all have been seen out in public and that his wife found him at your house at 4 am. You need not give the appearance of doing wrong." Tiffany understood her aunt's feelings, but felt as if Forrest did not want to help her and didn't want anyone else to help her, either. She thought he wanted to see her doing so poorly that she would come back to a marriage that was little more than slavery on a roller coaster filled with great memories from a distant past. When Tiffany kept telling her attorney that she loved Forrest, but wanted to be protected physically, and wanted to be sure he would not molest their child(ren), her attorney, who specializes in protecting children, told her, "you can write all of the love letters you want to him. But Forrest is sick. You can't fix him. The doctors can't fix him. And if prayer can fix him, I'll join your church." Ouch!

People talk. People gossip. They talked about Jesus. The popular saying "WWJD" or What Would Jesus Do? looks nice on key chains and bracelets, but when someone tries to do what Jesus would actually do, they often get hammered in the face. Tiffany tried to endure her cross, only to be met by image-conscious family members and a husband who, by no fault of his own, could not see past his own limited world view, and church and community members who wanted to live on their genitals and think that whenever people get together that it is about sex. Mr. Duke tried to help Tiffany the way he had helped other women at the church, old and young, widowed and married. He helps his daughter, but he is not having an affair with *her*. He helps the bishop's wife and daughter, but what of that?

When it comes to seeking a life of peace, self-image may not be the first thing that comes to mind, but it is important as one of our first tasks to seeking a life of peace and joy. Many women perceive self-image as something which is utterly unimportant to our spiritual lives. Others elevate the status of image as second only to God.

Breaking Out Of The Mold

We can learn a lot from Tiffany's portrait. This princess broke out of the mold of the press. She broke out of the mold of silence in her family which said, "Keep things quiet and don't make waves, even if you are being neglected and abused. As long as it looks good, keep it quiet."

She broke out of the mold of wife as martyr. She says, God did not tell her to be a door mat or to be choked half to death or to simply exist in an unhealthy system because her material needs will be met. She broke out of the mold of selling sexual favors for material gain, the oldest profession for women, because she knows that her body is a temple of God. She broke out of the mold of defining every relationship based on sex and intimacy, because prayer, protecting and providing for her children, and hard work define her. She broke out of the mold of worrying what neighbors or anyone else thinks about her early morning schedule. She gets up while the dew is still on the roses, like the Proverbs 31 woman.

What Influences Our Self-image? What Causes Us To Choose The Dream Homes We Choose?

God and His Word should influence our image. If we "meditate on the Word day and night and are careful to do everything written in it, then we will be prosperous and successful" (Joshua 1:8). Prosperity in this sense, has little to do with material wealth; rather it has to do with prospering in the fruits of the spirit (love, joy, peace, patience, kindness, gentleness, goodness, and self control).

A woman who has little or no peace is influenced by what the world (or popular culture) says to her. She is pressed. She, for example, does not breastfeed her children because she does not make the time and because it may ruin the shape of her perfect breasts. (She does not know that God gave her milk ducts and breasts to nourish and nurture her children. Or she knows it, but is more concerned about her figure or chasing a dollar.) God wants us to honor our parents, but we will never have peace if we live to be a trophy or an award for our parents.

MOTIVES AND SELF-IMAGE

God simply wants us to bring Him glory. God knows our hearts and He knows what we will say before we even speak. But sometimes our prayers are hindered because we have the wrong motives. For example, if you pray for a dream house so that you can show off in front of your siblings, you may get it and be house-poor and unhappy, or you may not get it because of your motives. Some folks ask for a gift so that people will praise them when God wants the glory. God wants us to cast off the old man. God wants us to walk in truth and healing and peace and joy, which is not based on what others think of us. God wants us to honestly look at our true motives, how much we rely on public opinion to motivate us, and deal with our self-image issues in order to pave the way to a future of peace and abundant joy.

QUESTIONS AND STATEMENTS TO CONSIDER:

1. Why do I do what I do everyday? (Do you clean your floors so people will say your house is clean, or do you clean them because you want God to know you appreciate the home He has graced you with?)

2. Do you take notes at church because you want to study later and become more intimate with God, or do you do it so others will think you are diligent?

3. Do you have children because your parents and in-laws want grandchildren or because you want to rear another generation which will serve our beloved Lord?

4. Are you afraid to do something right because it might *look* wrong?

5. Are you aware that we cannot win this world beating anyone over the head with a Bible? We will win them by showing Jesus in our actions. (James says that we show our faith by what we do).

6. Are you who you are or are you who people perceive you to be?

7. What can you do to put image in perspective?

Matthew 5: 13-17 says that the way we live as Christians says a lot to the world. The world hungers for the unconditional love of God which is so powerful that it causes me not to allow what people think to paralyze me or to inflate my ego, but at the same time, sister friends, it causes me to live in a manner that brings glory to God. If I know that my hands are clean; and God knows my heart, motives, and intentions, then I can walk in His power, might, and peace.

Matthew 5: 16 says, "Let your light so shine before men that they may see your moral excellence and your praiseworthy noble and good deeds and recognize and honor and praise and glorify your Father who is in Heaven." We who are in love with God and seek peace, know that, in spite of our struggles, we have to be a light in this dark world—a world where *some* students in public schools throughout America worship Satan and wear black robes or trench coats to school, where prayer is a problem, and where nobody wants to testify because they are concerned about what others will think. You hear my public testimony but only God and a whole lot of angels really know what I struggle with.

We have got to wake up! If we are to live as princesses in blessed peace, we have to walk under the direction of the Master Conductor. If life were a symphony and I were a harp, I would need to follow the direction of the conductor. All around me, I hear CB radios, AM radios, cassettes, CDs, cable, public television, *The New York Times*, *The Los Angeles Times*, and all of the noise in between. I hear the stock market quotes and the global market predictions, the daycare dilemmas and the health care situation. I hear of those who are hungry and of those who have died. Sometimes I am hungry; and sometimes death leaves and empty hole in my life. But, if I were a harp, my job would be to listen to the conductor, because in life there are a lot of great causes and issues and plans, but I have to listen to the conductor in order to know what my function is for each selection and season. I don't know about you, but I want to listen to God and try to live up to what He says for me to do with my time and what He says for me to do with my talents. I want continue to operate in blessed peace and joy by being a light in this dark world, but at the same time I know that when I do fall short (Romans 8:26 says we have all sinned and fallen short of the glory of God), that I can be redeemed, redirected, and still operate in His plan for my life because of what Jesus did at Calvary's tree.

After we have accepted Christ, the devil, God's enemy wants to keep us from understanding and walking in the unconditional love of God (which gives me peace and joy) and from being effective in the plans God has for our lives. I am redeemed. I am a light. I am a princess. I celebrate each moment. No matter what you repented of on Thursday or Sunday or Wednesday night, God has forgiven you; and you are a light. You are a princess. You live in a dream house. You simply have to tap into that which God has already given you. You are blessed when you can shake off what people say because pressed people have standards that are built on accumulation and presentation: How much does she have? Does she own her home? Did she earn a degree? Oh yeah? From where? You sure? And what does she look like? Is she fat? Is her husband gay? How does she dress? Does she vacation? That is all noise.

Listen to the Master Conductor. God orders our steps in His word. Have you ever been to Bermuda or St. Thomas or Paris or even a horse ranch and seen couples having such outrageous arguments over, for example, who will take the picture or whether they have paid the stable fee or not? It is not about the photograph or the fee—it is tension, turmoil, stress which mounts up, builds up, piles up, until one day, it explodes.

Every freezer has to defrost, whether it is at the altar at church on your knees, at the side of a trusted spouse, friend, prayer partner, therapist; or it could even manifest itself in a fit of violence or self-destructive behavior such as drinking alcohol, gossiping on the telephone, using prescription and non-prescription drugs too frequently. God wants us to live in peace and joy and be blessed, not loaded down with a whole lot of what would have been, who walked out, what ifs, when this happens I am going to do this, and if only I didn't do that. He knows we are not perfect, yet He does not condemn us. God wants us to let go of guilt and form and fashion.

When we walk in what God says is right, through His Word, through prophecy, through revelation and through prayer (listening), repent and accept repentance we live in the things dreams are made of. I tell our young son, Ollie, "everyone makes mistakes, even grown-ups." God wants us to be blessed, and the *Amplified Bible* describes blessed as "enjoying enviable happiness, spiritually prosperous— with life-joy and satisfaction in *God's favor* and salvation, regardless of his outward condition" [emphasis mine].

When we live for Christ, we will be persecuted. We will have tough times. Sometimes people will talk about you. I can't judge, but just using my sanctified imagination, I would say that they talk about you because they don't understand you. The pressed don't want to understand themselves. They do not like you because they have not tapped into their Divinity, and they do not like themselves. You are a light in this world, and sometimes you sin; the light flickers, but it is not consumed. The winds will blow and the light is not consumed. You are a princess. You are a light. Tap into it and shine! And if you want to spend your whole life worrying about what this one thinks, what that one wants, this one's fifty-year-old baggage, and if you're too fat or too lumpy then you will spend your whole life flickering in the press. You are a light—a bright light. Shine, sister friends, Shine!

The Sea Farer, our Virginia river house, is located on a dead-end street, nestled in between some of the finest homes on the most expensive property in the city. Our next door neighbor has a street named for his family. The ducks and birds roam the property. The lawns are all neatly manicured, but only God knows what actually goes on behind each front door. I left the Sea Farer, in all of its splendor, because although the front door looked nice, it was not worth the price I had to pay in the press. There will be conflict in any relationship or marriage, but I left the river house in all of its material splendor and the image (which had the illusion of being a dream house) as a response to the call on my life for peace and joy, in spite of the front door, the illusion.

I know that the Bible says that God hates divorce, but a princess knows that if the Bible were God's last word He would not use times of meditation and prayer, sermons, Bible teachers and books like these to speak to us today. Time in meditation taught me that although I could not undo the past, I could appreciate and accept only good things: health, safety, peace and abundant joy in the present moment. Princesses celebrate the moment.

We are all on a journey; and this book project coupled with meditation and listening to God, spending quality time with Him, has caused me to look beyond my own front door. No matter what popular opinion says, I am a princess. No matter where I live, because of my consciousness, river or no river, glitter or no glitter, it is a dream house, not constructed by men and women, but designed by a Father who loves me unconditionally and forever.

Even when our mothers and fathers forsake us (as in Tiffany's portrait), God, our loving heavenly Father is there. Jesus said, "Whoever does God's will is my brother and sister and mother" (Mark 3:35). Pressed women are so satisfied with being pressed, with being fueled by those outside of the will of God and their opinions—so satisfied with the imperfect, that they do not allow God to issue in the perfect.

God is our heavenly Father, and no matter what it looks like to those who look at the front door, we are called to operate out of faith in a God we cannot see rather than OPO (Other People's Opinions) which we can see and hear and feel. God is perfect and never changes. OPOs change every day. As soon as you leave the room, often those who remain have a commentary on you. Come on, now, whether you live in a trailer, a shelter, a river house, or the state house, do not allow yourself to sacrifice sweet peace and joy for an image. Or you will live in the press.

We are the only ones who know what is behind the fronts that people see. A lot of women front or talk themselves up: "my hair used to be like is this…" "my child did that…" and every time someone tries to tell them something, they rush them through it so they can recount a similar experience of their own. Aside from Our Beloved Lord, we are the only ones who know, and we are the only ones who genuinely care. We need to stop frontin' and get real. That is the only way we can ever begin to unlock our true motives and claim our royal inheritance.

Unlocking My Motives

A very important part of the front door is the key hole; that is what makes it different from every other door. What motivates us to do the things we do and see the world the way we see it? What turns our door knobs? Is it money? The adoration of others? Fame? The approval of our parents or in-laws? Recognition? Status? In order to live a life of peace and joy, I have come to learn that God and His will for my life must motivate me.

What motivates me to write so intimately to you is not recognition or setting any record straight; rather my motivation is based in what I can do to help advance the Kingdom. Let's unlock the door.

Once the door is unlocked, using the right key, the right motivation, there stands a woman of character who lines up in five ways (attitude, money, service, adversity, love) with the image she projects to the world, on the other side of the door.

OPENING THE DOOR OF MY CHARACTER: LET THE LITTLE CHILDREN COME TO THE PLAYROOM

A woman at peace and joy is a woman whose character reflects child likeness. When our son's friends visit, they do not inspect the house, take inventory or make mental appraisals of my china, crystal or African American art collection. They head straight for the playroom. They are light and unencumbered. In Mark 10:13, little children were coming to Jesus and some of the disciples began to rebuke them because it was not dignified or was not the way things were done. Jesus said, unless we receive the Kingdom as little children we will not enter it. Once we accept Christ, we are saved, going to heaven. But Jesus came so that we could have life and have it more abundantly. Abundant peace and joy are partially derived from child likeness. Children don't know about keeping secrets or protecting images. My neighbor's son once said, "my grandfather takes his teeth out at night."

A princess is childlike because she is humble, forgiving, loves unconditionally and does not hold grudges. She is not neurotic about her weight, height, breast size, hair texture, the model or year of her automobile, her address, or what someone else has or does not have. She has an imagination, can dream, and trust. She trusts in God, just as a child actually believes that London Bridge is falling down, falling down or that Miss Mary Mack actually pushed an elephant over a fence.

This reminds me a lot of my late friend Nellie Johnson, or Mother Johnson as the entire town of Tunica, Mississippi called her. I first met Mother Johnson while working to raise money with other student leaders in 1986. At the time, Tunica, which is now a gambling oasis, was cited as the poorest county in North America. Many residents had no plumbing and had to dumb their sewage in a canal which came to be known as "Sugar Ditch." On one of my many visits to Tunica, the television program "60 Minutes," Rev. Jesse Jackson and other activists were there to bring the world's attention to this area, which seemed to have been thirty years behind the rest of America.

Although Mother Johnson spear headed much of the local activism, and spiritually and physically fed many of the local and visiting leaders, she would literally hide when the cameras came. Her motives were not to be recognized by the world, but they were pure and childlike. She just wanted and loved justice. She was the archetypal princess: childlike, about her Father's business, and not caught up in the image game. I lodged at her home each time I came to town. She would cook and spoil us. (She would even mail home-made cakes and food to me while I was a divinity school student). I can recall her sweet grin and the way she would bubble with joy as she would clutch a green cup and say, "This is the cup Rev. Jesse Jackson drank from." Let the little princesses come and live in peace for heaven on earth belongs to them.

THE COLOR OF MY PEACE IS NOT GREEN

A woman at peace and joy is a woman who puts money in its proper perspective.

Some decorators and holistic health consultants argue that colors and aromas have mood altering effects, such as white opening things up, and blues and lavenders as calming, tangerine for livening things, up and the list continues. We can paint our homes any color, but if we do not have the character to line up with the truths in the Bible, the color does not matter. Your living room may be green, like the one in my childhood home in Hampton, Virginia. Color does not determine peace and joy. The color of a peace is not green—as in money.

If we think we can read *Dream House*, pray, fast, and implement the disciplines in this book, and then go out and buy a two million dollar house then we miss the point of this book in particular, and of self examination in general. We have to have a perspective on money and material things which is parallel to that of Jesus Christ. In the fourth Chapter of Mark, Jesus was suspected of trying to accumulate wealth to perhaps lead an insurrection against the Roman Empire. While the Pharisees kept a lid on the community, Jesus talked about the deceitfulness of wealth in His parable of the sower. Jesus wanted everyone to know that money is *not* what He was about.

If we want to live in peace we can not be like the pressed women with "green eyes" who live, eat, sleep, and breathe on what they can buy and how much they can stock up. No! We are princesses, those who say, like Jesus, "my focus is on the Kingdom; money and material things will not hinder my purpose, consume my thought life, and impede my spiritual growth"—everything in proper perspective.

Laws can break us, when we break them. Specifically, the Law of First Things, can cause us to bring about curses on our finances. In the Old Testament book of Malachi, chapter three, believers are instructed to "...bring all of [your] tithes and offerings into the storehouse so that there will be meat in my house." The Lord says, "test me in this, and I will open the windows of heaven and pour you out a blessing that you will not have room to receive."

If you want to know what is important to a person, look at their calendar and their checkbook. A princess has peace and joy, and not enough room to receive her blessings because God is first in every area of her life, including her finances. A princess gives cheerfully to God, the first fruits of all of her increase—a tenth plus an offering of her *gross* income— whether it comes to her in the form of a pay check, a gift or a love offering. She knows that God does not *need* her money. The kingdom can advance without her two dollars or twenty thousand dollars; but as she operates in first things, she cheerfully and obediently gives her first love her first fruits. I believe that the tithe is volatile; if we do not give it, the rest of our money will be under a curse. We cannot be in touch with the Divinity within us if we do not put Him first in every area. This is critical because many of my beloved are pressed because of money. Peace has nothing at all to do with money. The "American dream," to many is to burn a mortgage. I thank God that princesses are not limited to such a material standard. I lived in a situation where I had all of my bills paid, unlimited time with my child and husband, Prada, FUBU, Armani, DKNY, and the ability and flexibility to travel any where at any time. My peace comes from a God who lifted me out of that to a more "average" lifestyle, but since my peace and joy were not built on those things, I still have them—even without the excess.

The color of peace is not green. Money does not bring peace; however, a woman of peace and joy, a princess, puts in perspective.

Tah-da! I've Finished Cleaning (Let My Service Speak For Me)

A woman at peace and joy knows that faith is more important than "good works" but she serves out of love, calling, and obedience to God. Some folks do not have a call on their lives to serve in a general sense, but you may serve your neighbor by bringing in her recycling bin each week or taking photographs at her son's graduation and presenting them as a gift.

As we examine our motives in the context of service we know that others see us receive the volunteer of the year awards or the PTA Mom awards. Congratulations! (Really, it *is* hard work!) But here we ask ourselves, why are we doing what we do? Visitors see the clean house, but do we keep it clean so people will not think we are nasty (the pressed) or because we want God to know we appreciate our homes (the princess)? Being a princess, living in a dream house is about perspective. In this instance the princess has joy because she cleans (serves) with a song on her heart, while the pressed cleans be grudgingly saying, "I am so sick of dusting this house, if they want to see better homes and gardens, let them get a magazine!" The pressed don't think about women like those I saw in Egypt who stood in front of their homes waiting for a man to come by to pay them for sex so that they can buy food for their children.

My sisters who are poor in Egypt, in America and throughout the world wish they could serve their children food while the pressed complain about serving their children. Can you hear them? "I am not going to have a birthday party every year for those kids, that roof over their head is their birthday and Christmas!"

Think about it. Do we visit the sick so we can say we visited them or do we visit them to bring joy to their lives? When we clean our homes, folks see the finished product. Ta-dah! But they don't know what went into labeling the shoe boxes (only in America!), creatively cramming sixteen suitcases into one closet, scrubbing the cranberry sauce stain from the carpet, arranging the photo albums (and dating the photographs), and cleaning the aquarium at 1:00 AM. In other words, a lot goes into cleaning the home, whether we do it or someone else does. Service is like that, too. Folks see us receiving the awards. They read the feature articles and the write ups in the community newsletters, but they don't see all that went behind it. Therefore, if we don't enjoy what we are doing and are doing it for the wrong reasons, then we will be pressed.

We were created to give of ourselves; the greatest servant of all was Jesus Christ. But let's make sure our motives line up with our service. Don't join the church usher board so you will have the first opportunity to flutter in front of all of the single male visitors—join because you are called to serve as an usher and because you enjoy doing what ushers do and you will be peaceful and joyful.

We are not to love the praise of men (John 12:43), selfish recognition (Matthew 23:6) or anything more than God.

When A Dead Bolt Is Not Enough (Nobody Knows The Trouble I See)

A woman at peace and joy has a perspective on adversity which helps her listen to God, learn from her burns, and rebuke any bitterness which may accompany her rock or hard place. Does anxiety drive and motivate you? Do troubles take you over? When we move to a new home, we change the locks and determine not to let anyone in who might steal our belongings. Well joy is one of our belongings; peace is another of our belongings. As I princess, I am determined not to let anyone or anything, not things past (like hard times, hard history, sins committed, or sins visited) nor things present (like fruitless habits, the behavior of other people and institutions, the blessings and burdens of being a responsible family member and good citizen, dishonesty in business) nor things to come, break in and steal my joy. I live in the moment, celebrate the present, and do not look to the past or the future. As the songwriter penned, "this joy I have, the world didn't give it to me, and the world can't take it away!"

When we go on holiday do we fret the entire time because we think someone might break into our homes? Or do we enjoy the vacation knowing that we have the door locked, dead bolt locked and an alarm? Most people have more than one lock on each door. Sometimes one dead bolt is not enough.

As we continue to examine our character, let's look at how we deal with adversity. The Bible teaches that the devil, God's enemy, came to kill, steal, and destroy. God has a great plan and purpose for your life; and the devil wants to break in and prevent you from fulfilling it, and prevent you from experiencing the unconditional love of God.

The princess lives in peace because she has more than one lock on the door to her peace and joy. She screams, "Don't let nothin' or nobody steal your joy...lock it up!" Her dream house has several locks, which include prayer and meditation, exercise, therapy and perspective.

Prayer is divine communication with God. It includes praise, thanksgiving, confession, intercession (praying for others), petition (praying for personal prayer needs) and listening (meditation and transcendental meditation). The pressed, if they pray at all, go straight to petition, "Lord, bless me and give me this, that, and everything else I need."

Princesses praise and thank God; confess their sins, which means agreeing with God about sin. Then they pray for others as Scripture commands. They pray for other believers, those in authority, for the sending forth of laborers, for those in trouble, and for whomever and whatever God puts on their hearts. Then, most importantly, princesses, listen to God. The pressed do not want to listen to God because when we listen to God we are called to obey. What an awesome responsibility! Pressed women do not want to hear what God has to say because they are busy trying to figure things out on their own. They often have a word for the whole world, yet they cannot pray themselves through situations. Jesus wants us to pray and love Him through the good and through the difficult times (Matthew 26:31-35).

Princesses exercise, not only for the physical benefits of remaining healthy and flexible, but also for the physiological effects. It helps to relieve tension, I have found, especially in times of adversity. When I swim hard or do aerobics hard, my body releases endorphins which give me a natural high. When I exercise hard and boost my heart rate I often experience what is called "hitting the wall." When an athlete hits the wall she or he experiences extreme fatigue. The body wants to quit, but the mind wants to continue. Millicent Thompson taught me that the spiritual application here is that as princesses, we cannot let the flesh (physical body) cancel the goal of running the race or fulfilling God's divine purpose. The flesh says quit, give up, live in turmoil, figure it out yourself, but the spirit says, "you are more than a conqueror because of God's love." The princess exercises as one way to help to deal with stress and adversity because she knows that we all have stress, adversity and hard places.

A third support is therapy and support groups. Let me caution you first, sister friends, not to walk in the counsel of the ungodly. How can you seek counsel about your depression from Aunt Ina who has never been happily married, cried and slept through her children's adolescence, is in denial about her daughter's sexual molestation, and has a thankless and unforgiving spirit? Although the only ones who can judge are those who have all of the information, and those whom God has called to judge, princesses, pray for a spirit of discernment when seeking Godly counsel whether it is through counseling and therapy or a support group. The princess says, "if it is not coming from God, it is not coming here."

Finally, perspective is critical in adversity. Instead of asking, "why me?" princesses ask in every situation, "what can I learn from this?" I believe that God permits or causes every situation in order to translate us to a higher realm; and when we engage in pity parties, the only ones who are there are the devil and all of his fallen angels.

IS THE DOOR ON THE HINGES? LOVE: THE GREATEST OF THESE

A woman at peace and joy knows that love is above any law or principle. For she is called, we are called to: "love the Lord your God with all your heart, soul, and might. And love your neighbor as yourself." Jesus was held to the cross, not by nails, not by ambition, not by what he had obtained through scholarly encounter or life itself, but by love. Paul said to the church at Corinth, "if you know everything about everything, but have no love, you have nothing." (paraphrase I Corinthians 13).

What God's Word Says About Love

God loves us.	John 3:16
We are to love God.	Matthew 22:37
Because God loves us, He cares for us.	Matthew 6: 25-34
God wants everyone to know how much He loves them.	John 17:23

God loves even those who hate Him; we are to do the same.	Matthew 5:43-47; Luke 6:35
God seeks out even those most alienated from Him.	Luke 15
You love God when you obey Him.	John 14:21; 15:10
God loves Jesus his Son.	John 5: 20; 10: 17
Jesus loves God.	John 14:31
Those who refuse Jesus don't have God's love.	John 5:41-44
Jesus loves us just as God loves Jesus.	John 15:9
Jesus proved his love for us by dying on the cross so that we could live eternally with Him.	John 3: 14, 15; 15: 13, 14
Jesus wants our love to be genuine.	John 21: 15-17

Even if the door is locked, if the hinges or rusted or in disrepair, thieves *can* break in and steal. Love is the hinge on the door. Is your door half way off of its hinges? I don't know about you, but I am tired of pressed, nasty Christians. Betty told me about a great teaching church in North Carolina with a variety of programs for youth. She, her husband, and their daughters went to worship at First Calvary Church.

"The praise and worship, preaching and teaching are phenomenal," she said as she preached part of the sermon back to me over the telephone. "But we don't feel at home there; it is not child friendly" she said as the tone of her voice changed. She described a bossy, rude, nasty, pressed usher who caused her to feel uncomfortable. I thought, how sad for a pastor and his wife and family to allow God to use them to build such a necessary ministry—then some pressed woman drives off potential disciples. See how the devil uses pressed, church going, service-oriented, saved folks to try to dismantle the kingdom and discourage believers? "Faith, hope, and love abide, but the greatest of these is love" (I Corinthians 13). The door is off of the hinge, off of the hook, without love.

CHAPTER THREE

"If The Walls In My Living Room Could Talk, What Would They Say?"

A Blueprint for Examining My Relationships

We are to love one another (John 13: 34, 35) and demonstrate that love. (Matthew 5:40-42; 10:42)

Principle: In order to live in peace and joy, my relationships must not be the basis of my existence and they must show the love of God and reflect His design and perfect will, thus I choose to edify and encourage the people in my life.

Confession: My relationships and conversations build others up and reflect the love of Christ. The bread of gossip, criticism, and judgment I do not eat.

WHO SITS ON MY SOFA?

A woman at peace and joy does not base her happiness on her relationships with other people for she knows that everything she needs is inside of her dream home (her heart). Princesses ought to be careful about whom we allow to sit on the sofas in our homes, whom we allow to make a place in our lives. When a guest enters your home or a person enters your life, you ought to exercise caution when you say, "make yourself at home." You have no clue as to what "home" means to them; and you could literally turn your dream home (your heart), into a nightmare if you allow certain spirits to hang over and rub off on you.

From the perspective of a social scientist, women often define themselves by their relationships, saying, I am Romayne and Rosa's granddaughter; Gaye and Ollie's daughter; a partner in parenting with Myron; Tiger's (Ollie's) mother; Adil, Lisa, Kim, and Gayle's sister; Charles, Van, Oscar, Jacqui, Fleta, Lonnie, Billy, Richard, Ronald, Odessa, Yvonne, Pearline, Connie, Vannie, and Inell's niece; Deborah, Luvenia, Joy, Michael, Robert, Jeanne, Mother Shirley, Tobi, Kim, Keisha, Jennifer, Malverna, Dorothy, Marvin, Virginia, Jo, Karen, Carole, Ophelia, Andrew, Teri, Sharon, and Robert's friend; Rejhina, Tereyia, Richard, Ramon, Quintina, and Asha's godmother; Marie's god-daughter; Sister, Leslie, Kytti, Cyndi, Erica, Richard, III, Butch, Katrina, Buck, Dale, Lonnie, Gayle, Greg, Christine, Brian, Yuka, Taichi, Jeff, Monica's cousin; Leah, Sterling, Carmen, Lauren, and William Arthur's aunt. I love them all dearly and say many prayers for them, but they do not define my destiny nor do they know me the way God knows me.

Many people sit on the sofas of our lives, and enter the intimacy of our private spaces because we are relationship-oriented, fellowship-driven creatures. So, we ought to love and be in right relationship with those with whom we are in community, but should not let them define us or God's design for our lives. Otherwise we will be becoming pregnant because mom wants grandchildren or studying to become a surgeon because that is what dad wished he could have done or acquiring breast implants because our beaus and husbands are obsessed with bosoms.

We need to ask ourselves, "what type of influence do these relationships have on me?" You love and honor your sister, but if she is never happy, can't hug, always speaks badly about and threatens to leave her husband, why would you allow her to influence your marriage when you and your husband have determined to have a lifetime contract? Consider this, my sister friends.

STRAIGHT FROM THE ART GALLERY: A CROWN ON HIS HEAD (BLESSING YOUR HUSBAND)

A woman at peace and joy is one who recognizes that co-laboring and harmony are essential to the marital home. The married princess is a crown on her husband's head. According to Proverbs 31, she brings her husband good, not harm, all of the days of his life. She prays, plans and submits. You may think I am taking women back twenty years by even using the word "submission," but Paul teaches in Ephesians that the husband should love his wife the way Christ loves his church and should be willing to lay down his very life for her. If the husband is one hundred percent loving, the wife is one hundred percent submitting. He loves his princess into submission. (Some theologians exegete this text and define submission as being in co-mission or as being in mission with.)

The married princess sees marriage as a triangle. The husband is on one end, the wife is on the other and God is at the top. The closer each partner gets to God, the closer they come toward one another.

HE WAS GOOD ENOUGH TO SIT ON MY SOFA

A woman at peace and joy does not view singlehood as a tragedy, but rather as an opportunity; and the men whom she entertains are equally yoked with her, spiritually. "There are no good men out there," one single mother of three told her pastor when he asked her when she planned to marry. "At least three of them were good enough for you to make children with," he replied.

A woman at peace and joy does not sneak around with men, allow them to use her, distract her, and worm their way into her space. If he is good enough to sit on your sofa, he is good enough to worship with you, pray with you and for you, encourage you and bless you. Many woman are intimate with men, who are not their husbands, and they have never even prayed with him. (I am not suggesting that prayer is a prerequisite to premarital sex. In fact, the Bible teaches us that sex is a gift which God gives to married people. I use this illustration to make a point which is real and hits close to home for many pressed women).

Whenever a friend tells me of a new acquaintance, my first question is, "Does he love God?" Some women are pressed because they are in relationship with someone who steals from them, robs them of their joy and their inheritance as a princess just because they have physical needs for affection, adoration, attention, or orgasm. We all need to be loved, but no one will ever love us the way God will. The good news is that the pressed can change. With God all things are possible.

FUSSIN' AT THE COAT CLOSET

A woman at peace and joy does not take her unresolved anger or personal shortcomings out as she disciplines her children. Have you ever looked at your coat closet and wondered why you couldn't jam the winter coats, leather coats, beach gear and caps in without that nagging "I won't close syndrome" (only in America)? Sometimes when we are caught in the press, we fuss at the closet door that won't close, we fuss about the smell in the kitchen because we don't have the time to determine its source, we fuss, fuss, fuss. Pick, pick, pick. Pressed women get upset with their children, and often what they see in their children is a pressed spirit which has rubbed off of them; for they reproduce their own energy. Ouch!

The princess speaks peace into her own consciousness. Jesus was asleep in the midst of the storm and the rest of the disciples were frantic. He said, "Peace Be still." Michael Kelly taught me that Jesus was not speaking to the wind and the waves, but to His own consciousness. The princess goes out and jogs, does some aerobic activity, goes to the oceans and yells or cries. And she spends time in the silence—listening to the King of Kings who is there to guide her. The pressed woman does not have time for all of that, so she takes her anger and frustration with life out on her children or whoever else is under her authority, defenseless, and in her space. She does not take the time to praise them or as the experts say, to "catch 'em being good." She only takes time to yell and find fault. You know her. She is the one who says, "say 'thank you'" to her son *before* he has a chance to even receive his gift. Pick, pick, pick. She continues to be pressed because discipline without love and relationship lead to rebellion. A rebellious child, cultivated by the spirit of his environment, does not blend well in a dream house construct of peace and joy.

Paul teaches the church at Ephesus that "Children, [should] obey [your] parents, in the Lord." Further, he says, "...parents *[do] not provoke [your] children to anger."* When I discipline Ollie, I pray about it before I approach him, spend time in the silence, talk to him, tell him what the Bible says, discipline him, then pray with him. Afterwards, I ask, "Why do I discipline you?" Since age two, he would say, "because you love me." I tell him, "If I did not love you, I would let you do what you want, say what you want, wear what you want, and eat what you want." Just as our heavenly Father disciplines us out of love and correction and an eye on the future, so do princesses discipline their children. The pressed, on the other hand do not pray, plan, or discipline according to the Word, they simply discipline out of anger, typically feeling, "I brought you in this world, I can take you out."

Displaying Mama's China

A woman at peace and joy honors her parents, prays for her parents, and has come to terms with the fact that they did the best they could given the circumstances, information, temperament, destiny and choices they had.

A woman at peace and joy makes every attempt to make peace with her parents, no matter how lovable or unlovable they are. As my spiritual coach, Michael Kelly says, "place them lovingly in the hands of the father and leave them there."

Eighty four per cent of the women I talked to while gathering data for this book, said they do not even have photographs of their mothers on display in their homes. For many of them, the pictures do not make for decorating dream homes and dream lives. Whether your mother was your ideal of perfection or whether you wish you had been reared by a different mother, she (and your father), did the best they could. You may not like her taste in china or her taste in anything—you may not want to display her china or her photograph; but if we do not learn to cultivate a perspective where we accept our parents for who they are and refuse to hold them for what they did or did not do, we will never learn to live in the peace and joy we deserve. People can only give what they have. People make mistakes. Parents make mistakes. People are human. Parents are human. Princesses believe that we have two families: the biological family we are born into and as my manager, Michelle Gilliam, says, the one we acquire because of what our heart needs.

PLEASE, DON'T TAKE MY DISH HOME!

A woman at peace and joy knows whether she has the gift of hospitality (and sharing) or not. If she does not have the gift of hospitality, she believes God to send angels to make up the difference, and help her to be creative. If she does have the gift of hospitality, she practices it, shares her home, material possessions, and food freely and without the expectation of receiving something in return.

If you are pressed and do not want to share, be loving, be hospitable, if you plan to count your silver before your guests depart, if you are that uptight, then don't entertain.

Don't be down on yourself and grieve yourself. Everyone does not have the grace for or the call to be hospitable. But for those of us who are called to be hospitable, we won't be pressed if we have a generous, warm attitude about it. Ever been to a function where someone counted how many shrimp you ate? Or after you left someone talked for an hour about, "Mr. so-and-so's wife must have filled that foil up with fish" and "who took all of those ribs?" If you aren't called to the ministry of hospitality, you will be pressed every time you entertain. And no matter how nice the china, or how rare the silver, the pressed atmosphere does not blend into the things dreams are made of.

Linda told me about a birthday party she took her four year old son to, at the home of a church member. For the second year in a row she took her son to a party an hour away where nothing started on time, the poor kid's parents fought about the film, the camera, the matches and the cake. It just was not fun because mamma was pressed. She counted every napkin and ordered her husband to rush any time it even looked like someone was going to put a glass down without a coaster. At the end of the day, does a stain on a table matter more than an atmosphere of peace and joy? When her husband left the room, this pressed woman said in a sarcastic tone as she prepared plates, "My husband is sooooo cheap. I wanted to serve beef, but *all* he bought was chicken..." The princess would have said, thank God I have a husband to be present and helpful; and thank God for the chicken!

This pressed woman could have had a party at a fast food restaurant or skating rink since she is obviously not called to the ministry of hospitality, two years in a row. And as the saying goes, "if mamma ain't happy, ain't nobody happy." Her nicely decorated, trendy, new, spacious home, was, on a natural level, an American dream home, but on a spiritual level it was not that sweet. It was uneasy and contrived, the way Linda describes it. When the children wanted to tug at the balloons, mama would panic and yell, "No, don't touch the balloons, wait until the other children come." It's as if, look, but don't touch. Pose for our son's birthday pictures, but don't get too comfortable. You've been to places where the hostess is pressed and stressed to entertain. RSVP: I'll pass on invitations from the pressed; I choose peace and joy not form and circumstance. The atmosphere is what helps to makes a home dream like.

I See What I Say

A woman at peace and joy speaks (and lives out) God's Word in every relationship. (Thank God we are under His grace, because even princesses say things we ought not say). In this section we learn to speak affirmations into our own lives and into the lives of those whom we love. I tell my son every day and every night, "God has a great plan for your life." I tell him, "You are wonderful. You have skills. You are awesome! You are special. You are one of God's great helpers."

"I can never get all of my clothes hung up at one time" or "I can't keep that kitchen floor clean to save my life!" Sound familiar? Well sister friends, we will see what we say in our homes and in our relationships. You didn't hear what I said. We will see what we say in each situation.

The pressed woman says, "I don't know if I am coming or going," and because words have power, she literally does not know whether she is coming or going. "My four daughters are terrible. My husband is lazy and he has them ruined. My son is going to have asthma and be lazy like my husband and I guess his wife will have to mow the lawn and rake the leaves like I do" says the pressed woman who speaks negative affirmations into her life. The princess doesn't say, "my husband is sick." She says, like Gilbert Thompson, "my husband is catching his healing." Or she confesses Scripture and says, "no weapon formed against my husband shall prosper" (Isaiah 54:17). It is not that simplistic, but princesses are at least aware that words have power. Someone can be killed because of what we say. Someone could be persuaded not to take their own life because of what we say.

What comes out of our mouth is power because words have power. Walking in peace and joy is partly derived from our words. Princesses covenant with God and say what the Psalmist said, "may the words of my mouth and the meditations of my heart be acceptable in thy sight..." (Psalm 19:14). The dream house and dream heart is inclined toward God without false professions. Whether we were at home, in the presence of his colleagues or relatives, I made it a daily habit to complement and make positive affirmations about my former husband. Even today, when he calls for Ollie I say, "Tiger, your wonderful father is on the phone." One morning Tiger was so engaged in his "Prayer Bear" video that he did not want to go to the phone to wish his father a happy birthday. I turned the video off, before dialing the telephone, and said, "God loves your father. He is a wonderful person." I then asked, "How do you think he would feel if you did not call to wish him a happy birthday?" "Sad," he said. He spoke briefly, but at least he wished him a happy day. That evening we said special birthday prayers for his father. If I were pressed, I would have been happy that he did not want to send wishes to his father. But the press is not a place where I live; and I am rearing our son to be a prince. My attitudes and words rub off on him.

Pressed women say whatever they think they should say or whatever they think someone wants to hear just to get through a situation. Jesus warns us against false professions, for no matter what we say, God knows our hearts. While a pre-teenager, a princess-in-training, our family visited my maternal Aunt Gay in Oklahoma. She served squash and was very proud of her presentation. I wanted to express my appreciation and falsely told her how much I enjoyed the squash. Why did I do that? I did not know my words had *that* much power. She loaded my plate down with squash; and I ate it all. Whew!

In Matthew 15:8, Jesus says Isaac was right when he prophesied about you [saying], "These people honor me with their lips but their hearts are far from me." As a princess, I endeavor to keep my heart lined up with what God says, not with what the world expects of me, then I can be comfortable knowing that "out of the overflow of [my] heart, [my] mouth speaks" (Matthew 12:34).

"Restore to me the joy of my salvation."
(Psalm 51:12)

PART

2

The Corrective Phase

*"Create in me a pure heart, O God,
and renew a steadfast spirit within me."
(Psalm 51:10)*

CHAPTER FOUR

Waxing The Floor With My Manicured Hands

A Blueprint for Examining What I Use to Sustain Myself

Principle: In order to live in peace and joy, I must be disciplined to sustain myself physically (drink clean water, eat plenty of vegetables, protein, fruit, get enough exercise and rest).

Confession: My body is the temple of God. I will eat healthy foods. I will not dig my grave with my teeth. I will exercise and rest. However, I realize that I will not live by bread alone but by every Word that proceeds from the mouth of God. I live on His word so when I turn down my plate and fast, I still have what is necessary to prosper. I value proper diet and nutrition, but I know that the main thing is keeping the main thing the main thing.

In Chapter Three we examined our relationships, how we do them and the words we use. As Jesus instructed one crowd he said, "Listen and understand. What goes into a man's mouth does not make him unclean, but what comes out of his mouth, that is what makes him unclean" (Matthew 15:10,11). Quite naturally the Pharisees were offended by this because they had constructed so many laws regarding which foods were permissible. Jesus had to break it down to Peter saying, "Don't you see that whatever enters the mouth goes into the stomach and then out of the body? But the things that come out of the mouth come from the heart, and these make a man unclean. For out of the heart come evil thoughts, murder, adultery, sexual immorality, theft, false testimony, slander. These are what make a man unclean; but eating with unwashed hands does not make him unclean" (Matthew 15:16-12).

It is clear that Jesus was more concerned about our hearts than what we use to sustain ourselves physically. So, princesses know where to place the emphasis. We know that we ought to keep the main thing, the main thing. However, when we have physical maladies, it can hinder our ministry and light in the world. When Jesus looked over the multitudes, he saw spiritual and physical darkness. If God were not concerned about our health, Jesus would have told Jarius, the ruler of the synagogue, "Your daughter will go to heaven anyway." Instead, He healed her and said, "She is not dead. She is asleep. Give her something to eat." In that same pericope Jesus would have allowed the woman with the twelve-year issue of blood to continue bleeding. Instead, he said, "your faith has healed you." Jesus could have told the ten lepers, "Go on and keep that leprosy because you are saved and are going to heaven anyway." So the emphasis is not on the physical, but no matter how many gifts, how much wealth, how much beauty we have, without health, we cannot perform and give God our best.

I could wax the floor with my neatly manicured hands or my natural, healthy hair, but as Paul says to the church at Corinth, "everything is permissible but not everything is beneficial. Everything is permissible—but not everything is constructive." (I Corinthians 10:23). He goes on to say in verse twenty-five, "Eat anything sold in the meat market without raising questions of conscience, for "the Earth is the Lord's and everything in it." I know that when we bless our food, God sanctifies it, but Jesus wants us to be wise as serpents. Consuming too little water and too much of certain foods will not keep us out of heaven, but it *can* send us there a lot quicker.

Lemonade In My Washing Machine?

A woman at peace and joy is a woman who drinks at least half of her body weight in ounces each day; she knows that seventy to eighty percent of her body is water. Humans are the only mammals who don't drink water. Not drinking water is just as careless as putting lemonade in the washing machine. The wash cycle will be complete but the clothes will be yellow, lined with sugar and attract ants. Rather than wearing clean clothes, we will have to go through the labor of rewashing them and getting rid of the ants. Wow! Why not just use water? Why not just drink water? I have never seen a cow drinking lemonade or soda pop. Got water? Carbonated drinks cause our bodies to become acidic. Acidosis is a major cause of disease. It takes about eight glasses of water to flush the acid from one carbonated beverage from our bodies.

Princesses know that just as they need good, clean water, in their washing machines, they need good, clean (filtered, distilled, or spring) water in their bodies. The devil, God's enemy, came to steal, kill and destroy. He will try to use acidosis and dehydration to steal from the work God has called us to do.

GASOLINE IN MY GARBAGE DISPOSAL: ARE YOU KILLING YOURSELF WITH YOUR FORK?

A woman at peace and joy is a woman who eats a balanced, low fat diet. I didn't know it then, but during my high school years, I was killing myself with my fork, digging my grave with my teeth. I was running to school, student government meetings, ROTC meetings, church meetings, worship, and to work. In between I would eat fast food, whatever was on special at the tavern where I washed dishes and bussed tables. I drank very little water; but God spared me, helped me to detox; and now I am eating to the glory of God rather than eating what tastes good and is most convenient.

Research into brain function reveals evidence that the emotions of love, joy, faith, fear, depression, and even our sense of purpose in life, are not merely attitudes created through our mind's thought process. They are actually produced and reinforced by biochemical activity within the brain which is directly related to dietary wellness.

We can get away with putting gasoline in the garbage disposal. It is a liquid and eventually, the odor *will* go away. Believe me, I know. I cleaned a paintbrush in the sink once. But the kitchen garbage disposal was not designed for discarding gasoline, it was just more convenient, more expeditious. I did not see the results, but somewhere it may have damaged a pipe, polluted a stream, killed a group of ducklings. I don't know. We can get away with constantly eating fast foods high in sodium, fat, and calories and low in nutritional value, but somewhere we may pollute our colons, clog our arteries, or set our hormones off balance. Why take a chance?

Beef and pork are fine, if you choose to eat them, but many today are more concerned with profit that they are with health. Therefore they inject hormones and antibiotics into the animals which is not necessarily beneficial. Many farmers are so busy producing crops and selling them that they do not rotate crops and the soil is depleted of minerals which our bodies need. I have found it helpful to supplement my diet of whole foods with natural supplements so that I can be my best for God.

Eating a lot of pork, beef, fried food, and dairy products will not keep us locked out of our dream homes, but we will not enjoy them as much if we have hardening of the arteries, congested respiratory systems and other sorts of physical maladies related to man-made, profit driven, processed foods. It will also cause us to be less effective in the earth.

Gilda called Susan everyday around 5 o'clock and asked, "what are you cooking for dinner, girl?" Susan says of her friend of five years, "She was excited about food, lived for it, and even seemed to become aroused when I ran down my menu to her." "Are you going to put gravy on it?" she would ask as if she were a child anticipating her birthday gifts. Princesses eat to live and eat to the glory of our heavenly Father.

Put Some Pep In Those Steps

A woman at peace and joy makes time to exercise. Sometimes I can just run the vacuum, then there are times when I need to break out the attachments and get in the crevices of the steps. Tiger once asked," Mom, what is all of that ?" as he pointed to the dust in the cracks of our carpeted stairs. With white carpet, you know my carpet fuzz shows when it's dirty. My attitude is that I don't eat off of the floor, so although I maintain as well as I can, it is not top priority for them to be clean enough to eat from.

Our bodies are similar to the stairs. We should not be obsessed with the perfect figure, but princesses are concerned about health. Each day we need some type of exercise. Then every once in a while, we need to work on specific areas. When Ester developed arthritis, she began to swim and specifically work on her joint support. We hear it over and over again, "exercise." Ask any healthy mature woman, and she will tell you about the benefits of exercise. If she doesn't exercise, she will feel it. It is not all about the sagging and the physical appearance; exercise has more to do with quality of life: peace, and joy.

The Carpet Will Dry Overnight

A woman at peace and joy knows when and how to rest. She knows that her mind and body heals and restores itself only when she rests.

"The carpet should be dry by morning," the carpet cleaner told me as he left our home. Nothing I could do, short of opening a window, would cause it to dry any quicker. I had to wait and I had to rest. Even God rested on the seventh day—not that He needed rest. He just wanted us to know that rest is important. "We are fearfully and wonderfully made" (Psalm 139:14). We were made to rest that we might become restored, mentally. So put your feet up while the carpet dries. We are not worthwhile because of what we accomplish nor are we only worthwhile *only* when we are accomplishing something. We are worthwhile because God loves us. Princesses know that they need rest.

CHAPTER FIVE

Too Much Static From The Attic

A Blueprint for Examining My Perspective on the Past

Principle: In order to live in peace and joy, I must put the past in perspective, line my prayers up according to it, and move on.

Confession: Today is a new day. My past is behind me. I chose to live in peace and joy this day.

WHAT'S IN THE ATTIC?

A woman at peace and joy knows that there are two types of things in her past: things she knows about (such as past joy, pain, negative events, sins committed, and sins visited); and things she does not know about, many of which are out of her control (such as generational sins and curses spoken against her).

Over the past six years, I have made it through the politics of a doctoral dissertation; testified in court against a trusted professor who was charged with assaulting and battering me; been admitted to a hospital after being bitten by one of the professor's relatives whom he molested as a child and suffers from multiple-personality disorder; lost a child; committed a beloved family member to a hospital and gone to therapy with them; bought a house; moved twice; separated from a spouse whom I love, and the list continues. That is just part of what is in my attic. During that same time I also wrote some of my most powerful poems; delivered some of my most life-changing messages; gave birth to a righteous son, nursed him on my breast, witnessed to him, witnessed his salvation and preaching ministry; forgave and released all of those who have hurt me or used me; became qualified as a professional speaker; toned my body back to my pre-baby size; and most importantly, I have become more intimately involved and in touch with God.

Everyone has baggage. Some people have trunks. Many of us, have a lot of junk in our trunks. But what separates the princess from the pressed is perspective. Princesses enjoy each moment and each day; while the pressed feel pitiful for themselves and have a critique on everyone else's blessing in order to minimize their own pain.

I Just Fixed That Attic Floor Board! (When The Pain Of The Past Comes Back)

A woman at peace and joy does not become paralyzed by the pain of the past, instead she learns from it and becomes stronger and more resilient. As a princess, I realize that all that is in my attic, the good and the bad, has caused me to be who I am, has made me more resilient, more dependent on God, and it all gives an occasion for testifying about God's unmerited favor.

Let It Go, Girl! (On Forgiveness)

Tyra Banks says, "the people you hate either don't know or don't care." UN forgiveness holds the pressed down. When we hold someone, we are only holding ourselves. Hate, stress, and unforgiveness cause emotional and physical stress which discounts the quality of our lives and also has physical manifestations. Princesses, live in dream homes because they can look in the mirror and honestly say, "let it go, girl."

Michael Kelly, taught me that everyone either expresses love or is crying out for love. When we look at people in this light, how can we hold them? James Byrd, Jr., the man who was dragged to his death on the back of a truck in Texas, has a family who understands this principle. His family issued a statement of forgiveness even prior to the convictions of his murderers. Had they not done so, they would have had to live with the grief of losing their beloved coupled with the grief of unforgiveness. I honor them for not focusing on the racial motivation of the crime or their own pain. They focused on reconciliation and love. How wonderful! How dream-like.

While working on my dissertation, I had an advisor who wrote on a draft of my dissertation proposal, "good work. Should get through the committee on degrees. Only a few typos." When we went into a meeting with my other two committee members, they had critical suggestions about my conceptual framework. My advisor, apparently insulted by his colleagues, took it out on me. I prayed and forgave him; and God made up the difference. Joe Maxwell, an ethnographer and committee member, *volunteered* to replace my advisor and the rest is history. If I had held my original advisor, I would be bitter, and would have probably taken the entire nine years to write my dissertation, rather than soaring. I completed it in two years and earned Harvard's Advanced Doctoral Fellowship for timely and successful academic progress.

There's A Sweet Spirit In This Place (On Resentment)

All women have resentments. It is what we do with them, and how we perceive them that separates the princesses from the pressed. If the narrator in Melville's *Bartleby, the Scrivener*, were a female, he may well have been a princess for he was able to reside in peace and joy by appealing to God even after having murderous feelings for Bartleby. The narrator referred to a type of resentment that led him to contemplate killing Bartleby. He said, "But when this old Adam (Demon) of resentment rose in me and tempted me concerning Bartleby, I grappled him and threw him off." The narrator cast off the demon of resentment which gave him the peace to appeal to a higher authority. How did he throw off the resentment? What saved him? He said He recalled the divine injunction: "A new commandment give I unto you, that ye love one another" (Words spoken by Jesus to His disciples. John 13:34).

"Love Keeps No Record Of Wrong" (1 Corinthians 13)

I don't hold white people for slavery. I don't hold the black men who think that the only place for a woman is on her back. For in my dream home, I refuse to hold onto anything that is not lovely, pleasant, outstanding, wonderful. In order to live in peace and joy, we cannot keep a record of specific harms and sins visited. God does not keep records of what we did. Princesses seek to be like God. If we keep our own records of wrong our dream homes would become more like junk yards.

What's Under That Carpet Anyway? (On Demystifying Generational Plagues)

A woman at peace and joy knows about generational plagues, and rebukes them from her life. She confesses and seeks forgiveness for her sins, and the sins of her foreparents and ancestors.

What is under that carpet in the attic, anyway? It is good to know what we have a propensity for so we can pray specifically and work hard to avoid certain areas where our roots show us there have been problems. One relative who was one of the nicest, most hospitable, neat, people you would ever want to meet, died, from what I remember being told as a teen, stooped over a trash can full of her own blood. She bled to death from complications related to alcoholism. She is neither the first or last alcoholic in my family, but knowing my history, I pray about and make decisions regarding drinking so that 20 years from now, I am not sittin' at a bar somewhere talkin' about what I could have or should have done in my life. I don't think it is a sin to drink, but I do not want to fall into a dependency where I am looking for a drink when I rise rather than looking for a Word from the Lord.

A six year old boy, charged with attempting to kill an infant was featured on a 1997 PBS special. The boy's uncle said, "every male in our family, from age 6 to 86 has an

assault and battery charge." Some families are six generations deep in alcoholism, insanity, incest, occult religions,
whether known or unbeknownst to them.

This section focused on generational curses and plagues
because we need this information in order to live in peace,
but I must thank God and a whole lot of angels that where
there is a down, there is an up. Where there is a south,
there is a north. Where there are curses, there are blessings.
Just as we have genetic and spiritual dispositions towards
all of the negative things of our families, we also have the
blessing of being able to walk in the favor and fortune of
our ancestors.

I know that it was the grace of God and the prayers of
my family and other saints that have kept me in my right
mind. I could have been dead in a drunk driving accident.
A.I.D.S. is the leading cause of death among African American, aged 25-44; I am African American, and on the
comfortable side of 35. Had it not been for God's grace, I
would have died from it, too. Thank God for amazing grace!

God's grace flowed from generation to generation in
my family. Tiger's, paternal great-grandfather was a preacher,
pastor, and businessman in Baltimore, Maryland in the
1950s. His paternal grandmother is a teacher and lay minister. His paternal grandfather was a church steward. His
father is a preacher, former pastor and businessperson. His
maternal great-grandfather, Ollie Bowman, Sr., although
functionally illiterate, could read the Bible, was a deacon
and president of the prayer band. His maternal grandfather, Ollie Bowman, Jr., the one he is named for, is an
Elder, worship leader, and Bible teacher. And he is the off-
spring of two ministers.

Tiger accepted Christ in March, 1998, a few months before he preached his first sermon. Three weeks before he was scheduled to speak at Briarfield Elementary School (in Newport News, Virginia) I said, "Tiger, I am praying for your speech at Mr. Ashby's school." "I am not going to give a speech, mama," he said with conviction. "I am going to preach." And he did! He quotes Scriptures, shares, sang with the church choir and visits the sick. One summer day, we lay on the deck and he looked up and asked, "Mom, when are we going to visit the sick? We haven't been this week." He didn't ask to go to the amusement park or to Chuck E Cheese's—not that day, anyway. He asked to visit the sick. Selah! I also know that our son has child molesters, batterers, and substance abusers in his blood line, we talk about it, pray about it and rebuke it all in Jesus' name. I teach him, "you will not touch other's private parts, and they will not touch yours." "If anyone does or says anything to make you feel uncomfortable, tell me, and I will believe you." I tell Ollie, "do not hit your mother, wife, girlfriend or any other woman unless you are defending yourself." "No drugs. No guns. No lying. No stealing." I am not going to wait until he is in front of a judge before I start teaching, training, praying and rebuking. If he is old enough to understand God's plan for salvation; his numbers in Spanish, English and Japanese; the plot on Nickelodeon's "Rug Rats"; several of my poems and Martin Luther King, Jr.'s, too, he is old enough to know about these things.

So friends, we can have peace when we pray about eliminating generational plagues and say with authority, "If it's not coming from God, it's not coming here." We can have joy when we see God's faithfulness to the third and fourth generations.

CHAPTER SIX

Takin' Out The Garbage

*A Blueprint for Examining
the Clutter in My Life*

Principle: In order to live in peace and joy, I must simplify my life and edit habits, attitudes, relationships and *things* that clutter my life, weigh me down and cause me to be less fruitful than I was created to be.

Confession: I choose today to eliminate and bring to no effect, all of the distractions that keep me from a life of peace and joy.

SANDING MY FLOORS: ON ELIMINATING SPLINTERS

A woman at peace and joy knows that she needs to exercise self control in eliminating habits that hinder her peacefulness and effectiveness.

We can walk on the unsanded hardwood floor. It supports us; it fulfills its purpose. But it is not the type of floor that makes for a dream house because if you are like me and walk without shoes, you may get splinters. So we can either eliminate it by covering it up, or by working on it. The unsanded floor works, but not as well as it could. It is better than nothing, but it is not in its best state. Many pressed women are hindered in their effectiveness and don't live in dream homes because they have habits that cause them to be diluted and misguided. They get by, but not as well as they could.

Do you feel edgy if you don't have your prescription pills? Are you anesthetized by antidepressants? If you smoke too many cigarettes, too much marijuana, take too many of your prescription pills and lie to your doctor, eat too many hormone and antibiotic-laced animal products, drink alcohol heavily, practice unsafe sex, use profanity regularly, put this book down, prop it up and do two things:

1. Tell God, that you can't do it, but you believe that He can!

2. Believe. Jesus said in Mark, "whatever you ask for in prayer, believe that you receive it, and it will be yours" (11:24).

Reframing My Portraits
(Eliminating Attitudes That Cause Bitterness)

A woman at peace and joy is a woman who can look at the light of God in other people in order to avoid bitterness or edginess. While in the Intercontinental Hotel gift shop in New York in the Summer of 1998, I encountered a white male in line waiting to purchase a newspaper. In front of him stood a black female digging through her change to make a purchase. The man became so impatient. He blurted out, "it was a lot better when *you all* had your own hotels." The sociologist in me thought, "Wow. How pitiful that this man has narcissistic entitlement." But I am no judge. I could have been upset about that all day; or I could have lived the rest of that year feeling as if I had to prove to white people that African Americans are entitled to the same things they are entitled to, but the princess in me put a different spin on it. I prayed silently for the man and for the poor girl who had to put up with such verbal abuse. Princesses reframe in order to keep peace and joy at the center. This morning after I took Tiger to school a Volvo in front of me caught my eye because I saw the word "rapture" on the bumper sticker. The sticker read, "when the rapture comes, I want your car." On the opposite side was an icthus with feet and the word "Darwin" written inside of the fish shape. Initially I felt empty, as if I were behind the devil himself. But all day, I have been praying for that driver and people like him or her. I did not personalize it, because "our struggle is not against flesh and blood, but against the rulers, against the authorities, against the powers of this dark world and against the spiritual forces of evil in the heavenly realms" (Ephesians 6:12). Therefore, as princesses, we are called to "put on the full armor of God, so that when the day of evil comes, [we] may be able to stand [our] ground, and after [we] have done everything to stand, [we can] stand firm then, with the belt of truth buckled around [our] waists, with the breastplate of righteousness in place and with [our] feet fitted with the readiness that comes from the gospel of peace" (Ephesians 6: 13-15).

You may have to take your mother-in-law's picture down in order not to feel disgust; but a princess would make it may be easier by reframing an old picture of her in her younger days with your then five-year-old husband. That way she sees her as a blessing who poured into the life of her soul mate rather than the neurotic, hypersensitive, dictator that she feel steals from her joy. The princess sees her mother-in-law, in this example as one crying out for love. A princess reframes rather than taking on spiritual issues and making them personal.

Princesses do not drive on their egos and get caught up in road rage. At the end of the day, who cares who got to the stop sign first? Both cars have to stop, anyway! While in Chicago, I saw a bumper sticker which read, "WARNING: I go from zero to bitch in five seconds." Reframe and "your grief will turn to joy" (Proverbs 15:30). When Imani spilled grape soda on my light carpet, she had tears in her eyes when she told me. "Accidents happen, just try to clean it up" I told her. "Even grown-ups make mistakes," I assured her. Ten years ago, I would have reacted differently. Reframing makes life more peaceful for us and for those who share our space. Others should not have to walk on egg shells in our dream homes.

I Can't Tell You Nothin' 'Bout Your Decor (Or Your Love Life)

A woman at peace and joy can honestly answer the question, "Why is he *in* your life?" I wouldn't come into your house and ask, "Why do you have that horrible wallpaper in the hallway? I am not attached to the wall paper. I don't love your wallpaper. Similarly, I wouldn't come into your life and ask, "Why do you have that self-serving, unholy man in your life?" I am not attached to him, either. If you want to live in peace, if you want to find joy, I can't tell you nothin' about your man, but please, think about it. We can't have dream homes, dream lives, with someone who brings us down. The pressed woman uses her man as an accessory to her life, like the marble paperweight with no paper under it—looks good, takes up space, but serves no positive or Divine function.

Here, I do not advocate divorce, but this is addressed to single women, divorced women, all women who cling onto any or every man in order to feel complete. When you have split ends in your hair, you may have to get up to three inches cut. Although your hair is healthier, you still miss those damaged ends because you were used to the length and styling flexibility. I have been eating natural foods and using natural cosmetics and self care products for the past thirteen years. It was not until 1997 that I decided to wear my hair natural. At that time it was down my back and past my breasts. But I knew in order to cut the permanent relaxer out, I had to start all over. So after I let about four inches grow out I went to a salon in Virginia Beach and had the rest cut. When I came home Myron said, "If they had cut off two more inches you would be like Demi Moore." (At that time Demi was sporting a very close, crew cut). Although my hair was short, it was thick, natural, easier to swim with, and a lot healthier than it was the chemicals. Whether it is a grooming decision or a decision to end a bad relationship, we feel a sense of loss, but the outcome is a lot healthier. It is not about the length of your hair; it is about how healthy it is—and ultimately, how healthy you are. Similarly, it is not about finding the right man; it is about *being* the right woman. Princesses hook up with princes: men of faith; men of relationship; men of resources; men of balance; men of agreement; and, most importantly, men of love. And they live happily ever after, so the story is written. Use this as a checklist, sister friends.

Country Charm For Country Bumpkin? (Kindness For Weakness?) The Art Of Not Letting Folks Get Over On Me

A woman at peace and joy know she was not created to be taken advantage of; rather, she is one who can turn and twist, still stand firm, and do what she was created to do. We may have to turn and twist, fast and pray, be strong, and stand up for ourselves, in the workplace, academy, church, home improvement negotiations, and every day encounters in order to eliminate the anger, physical and emotional tension caused by "telling someone off" at work or writing the Better Business Bureau about a company's unethical conduct.

Vannie Smith, a 64 year old minister and physician told me, "Every night at work, I have to work on not getting nasty." As she puts it, "I have buried two husbands, raised five children, and I am not going to have some 25 year old nurse disrespect me." Vannie is no doormat, so she does not have to lay awake wondering, "well, I should have said this," or "I *could* worship on Sundays, with my family, if only I would stand up for myself and tell my supervisor that I do not work on Sundays, I prefer to worship." She stands up for herself and tries to allow her light to shine simultaneously.

I Can't Get Hung Up In The Cob Webs: The Blueprint For Setting Boundaries

Some pressed women are people pleasers who burn out because they want to do something about *everything* they see. They revolve in a continual cycle of superwomen turned super sick! If I cleaned the cobwebs every time I entered my home, I would have to do it each time. I need to pray when I enter, take a deep breath (because you never know what the day or moment or season with bring) rather than sweeping cob webs with the side of my grocery bag on the way in the house. If I cleaned the cobwebs off of the driver's side mirror, I could become distracted and cause a car crash. You understand. We each have two hands and two feet and only twenty-four hours.

When we princesses can get caught up in other people's issues, struggles, webs, to the extent that we are fruitless in our own destinies, we transition and become pressed. I know there are a whole lot of amens out there on this one. Often motivated by approval or public opinion rather than God's love and divine purpose, the pressed are always tired and always have a long story about how someone wasted *their* time. Pressed women allow others to waste their time, rob from their destiny, and make each day less fruitful. And, once the sun sets, the day is gone—it's no dress rehearsal; this is real life in real time.

Jo Kadleck and I were eating at a cafe in Manhattan when up came a man whom I will call Pino. Pino came up to the table, bursted into our meeting and said in a loud, unsteady voice, "damn, you are fine!" Then asked, are you still married?" He seemed to have been intoxicated, and continued to talk and tell me about the movie he was helping to film in the adjacent hotel. Although I am often nice when folks think I should be mean, I simply did not have time to get caught up in this cob web. I told him politely that we were meeting and it was nice seeing him and that I would give his regards to Rejhina, the goddaughter we have in common. Had I gotten tangled in that web, he would have detained us, and I may not have finished collaborating with Jo on this book. When he departed, Jo asked, "do you know him?" I know him, but I do not owe him. My coach, Michael Kelly would be proud of me on this one because he has taught me to be firm, friendly, frank and fair, rather than just friendly and fair. It works!

PART

3

The Preventative Phase

"He will keep you in peace."
(Isaiah 26:3)

CHAPTER SEVEN

No *Guests* Allowed In The Bedroom

A Blueprint for Examining the Priorities of My Intimate Affections

The love between God and Jesus is the perfect example of how we are to love others. (John 17: 21-26)

Principle: In order to live in peace and joy, I must place God first and my husband second to all other relationships and things.

Confession: God is my first love. My marriage comes second to my devotion to God. All other calls on my life follow these.

THERE'S NO PLACE LIKE HOME (AND THERE IS NO LOVE LIKE GOD'S LOVE)

God must be our first love. (Matthew 6:24; 10:37)

A woman at peace and joy is one who puts God first. This is evident by the way she spends her time, money, and talents.

Wherever we are, wherever we call home, God is there. There is no place like resting and meditating and listening in the presence of God. Home is where God is. He does not change and He will never leave. Princesses are called to:

Love Him

Praise Him

Honor Him

Serve Him

Be Intimate with Him

Our intimacy can increase through: prayer ("I will always pray with joy" [Phillipians 1:4]), Bible study, praise, liturgical dance, consecration fasts and meditation. As princesses, *"we are not to love* the praise of men (John 12:43), selfish recognition (Matthew 23:6), earthly belongings (Luke 16:19-31), or *anything more than God"* (Luke 16:13) [emphasis-mine]. God wants to be your first love (Revelations 2:4).

THE (MARRIAGE) BED IS NOT DEFILED

A woman at peace and joy is a woman who prioritizes her marriage and brings her husband good, not harm, all of the days of his life. She is called to:

Love him

Pray for him

Honor him

Serve him

Be Intimate with him

I believe that women need love and security; love and protection; love and cooperation. Men, on the other hand, need love and sex. Princesses understand that sex is a gift which God gives to married people to enjoy. Adam and Eve, as God designed it, brought their beings of companionship, unity and delight together and were intimate; and this was some time before God commanded them to bear children (Genesis 3:16).

Husbands and wives have God's permission to enjoy sexual union; and they defraud one another when they deny each other such intimacy (I Corinthians 7:3-5). Even if a princess is not *in love* with her husband she knows that the revival of will is possible through Christ. The physical environment, timing, and attitude which she brings can help to influence lovemaking with her partner and make it something to truly praise God for. Any witnesses out there?

ON THE NURSERY BECOMING THE GUEST ROOM (CHILDREN: MINE ONLY FOR A SEASON)

A woman at peace and joy is one who understands that her children belong to the Lord; and she is a steward over them, only for a season. Her job is to train them up in the way they should go so that they do not get older and depart from the truth.

Pressed women put their children before God, and before their husbands. Your son is not your man! As mother/ princesses, we are like soft blankets; we need to cover our children, but not smother them.

While visiting a library in Tallahassee, Florida, a librarian complemented Tiger on his behavior and complemented me on the time it seemed that his father and I had spent rearing him. She then broke down almost to tears and said, "I was crushed when my children didn't need me anymore."

Life brings new seasons. Princesses pray for their children's spouses, for their independence and for their salvation. The pressed need their children to make them feel complete. Don't get me wrong, princesses value mother love and spend a lot of energy on the ministry of motherhood, but our lives revolves around God and the Divinity within us rather than around our children, or we, too will become pressed when we feel as if our children do not need us anymore.

Often when I watch the televised National Basketball Association drafts, I notice how many young men are there with there mothers. Two of my friends who are married to professional ball players have shared with me the way they feel as if they have to "compete" with their mothers-in-law. "It's as if she feels that I took her man and that I am living in the home *she* should be living in," Sierra said as she dropped her head and cried.

Pressed women manufacture this type of confusion when roles are confused. A princess praises God when her son finds a woman who will, "be a crown on his head" (Proverbs 31). In Chapter Nine, we will examine further, the ministry of mother love within the context of planning.

CHAPTER EIGHT

Potpourri And Praising

A Blueprint for Being Good to Myself

Principle: In order to live in peace and joy I must be good to myself, pamper myself, and praise my Creator at the same time.

Confession: I know that charm is deceptive and beauty is fleeting. And although my beauty comes from reverently and worshipfully serving the Lord, I take care of myself. And while I pamper myself, I praise my Creator.

Potpourri is a little something extra. So is pampering, but it is necessary. If I don't take care of myself, who will?

POLISHING AND PRAISING

A woman at peace and joy praises God for her eyesight as she applies her eye makeup, for example. She praises God for her toenails as she gets her pedicure; she doesn't wait until she has nail fungus or an ingrown nail to appreciate them. She praises God for toothpaste and proper dental care as she brushes her teeth, and for her hair itself and shampoo as she washes her hair.

BATHING AND BLESSING

A woman at peace and joy blesses every area of her body as she bathes. We are in the bathroom, now. A princess blesses and prays over herself as she washes. I call this ritual my Kingdom bath. I relax, light my Chi or lavender candle, and bless my temple as I bathe and soak.

CLEANSING AND CONFESSING

A woman at peace is reminded of the need to confess, agree with God about sin, cleanse herself spiritually with Living Water, as she cleans herself physically.

Most of us clean ourselves daily, but every now and then we have to do deep cleaning like facial scrubs, masks, and hair removal. Each day we confess, but sometimes we have to set ourselves apart, pray, and fast. I have found it essential to set myself apart daily, while the dew is still on the roses, and spend time listening to God, seeking my daily marching orders and committing my day to my Beloved Lord. Whether we are cleaning the floors of our dream homes or cleaning our pores, cleansing is imperative to cleaning our souls.

A woman at peace and joy is one who looks good, because her beauty is not skin deep, and she feels great because she loves herself and takes care of herself. Princesses realize that "charm is deceptive and beauty is fleeting, but a woman who fears the Lord is to be praised" (Proverbs 31). How can we be full of peace and joy if we are all broken down, unkempt, and wishing we had just spend ten more minutes at the mirror? It puts a little extra pep in my step. Whenever I had a test at school, I would wear a suit, no matter how tired I was; and it helped me feel better. I look at it like this, as a princess, I represent the King. I want to be like Princess Tiffany: beautiful on the inside *and* the outside. If they can look good out there (in the world), we can look and feel good in here (in the Kingdom).

CHAPTER NINE

Sittin' At The Computer

*A Blueprint for Examining My
Plan and Purpose in the Earth*

Principle: In order to live in peace and joy I must ask
God for and focus on a plan for my personal life and a
plan for my professional life. I must have a vision for
my life.

Confession: I pray more than I plan, but I plan so that
I might have peace and joy, fulfill my destiny and touch
my generation.

We're in the study now. Above my Power Mac, I
have a huge bulletin board affixed to the wall
with photographs of Tiger, my godchildren,
and friends, business cards, notes, and bumper stickers. One
sticker reads, "Life's a Joy....then you Ascend." Another
reads, "Thy Word is Truth" (John 17:17). One says
"Vineyard" (from Martha's Vineyard"), One says
"Hollywood." I also have a violence prevention bookmark
and a self esteem bookmark for children which are
surrounded by Tiger's artwork. On the right corner of my
board I have a bookmark which my dear friend Carole

Copeland Thomas designed, titled "Remembering my Mikey" (a tribute to her deceased, super son). I have a few business cards scattered below the African mud cloth boarder as well as two plane tickets which are penned under Bexar County Congressman Lamar Smith's newsletter. On either side of the board is African American framed art. One is of "The Banjo Lesson" the other is a Romare Beardon print. The sticker on my ink jet printer reads, "Something wonderful is about to happen." Those on my computer monitor read, "Smile, God loves you," "Jesus is Lord" and "computer." (The "computer" label is one of many labels I have taped throughout the house with names in Spanish and English since Ollie is very interested in words and reading). Whew! Lists for Tiger's school pictures are affixed next to my NSA logos, my Alpha Kappa Alpha Sorority button and a few miscellaneous phone numbers. A thick description of the rest of my study is not necessary because whether you are a princess or whether you are pressed, you are well aware of the many hats which Kingdom women wear, the many responsibilities we juggle, and the many people who depend upon us. With all of this, praying and planning are essential to the blueprint of any dream house, be it a dormitory room, a trailer, a room in a homeless shelter or a mansion with four wings.

While I was away working in New York, the 40 gallon water heater gave way at the river house in Virginia. I came back to a slushy family room, and guess what was floating on the water? It was the flood alert alarm which sounds at the first detection of water (from the heater). Well, I purchased and installed the alarm, but I was in another state when it sounded, maybe on Broadway at "Bring in 'Da Noise, Bring in 'Da Funk," maybe sleeping, maybe at the Motown

Cafe, maybe taking Tiger on a stroll down 5th Avenue, maybe at the Japanese bookstore looking for a cookbook which features Hijiki, maybe teaching for the Cathedral of Allen African Methodist Episcopal church in Jamaica, or maybe caught in the gay pride parade traffic in a courtesy car reading *Newsweek*. Either way, *I* did not hear the alarm. Who knows if it even sounded? (You know how that mail order merchandise is when it arrives—you're not sure it works, but it's not worth the hassle of returning it.) The point, sister friends, is that planning is critical, but as Jessica Kendall Ingram says, "we have to pray more than we plan" because all of the planning in the world cannot prevent some things. Our heater needed to be replaced, the carpet in the room was ruined, but I have peace and joy because as I discussed in Chapter Six, Takin' Out the Garbage, I reframed my attitude so that I would not become bitter. I clung to what Myron Howie calls, "an attitude of gratitude," which caused me to thank God we had the resources to get another heater, appreciate our hot water and being able to use the dishwasher more than I did prior to the temporary loss of hot water, and appreciate the fact that the water did not cause electrical damage or a fire. An added bonus was that all of the mess compelled me to clean the den in great way.

QUERYING THE MASTER ARCHITECT (FINDING YOUR DESTINY)

A woman at peace and joy asks a series of two questions, and follows with deep meditation in order to seek a sense of destiny and purpose in her life. First, she asks God, "what is your plan and purpose for my life?" Listening, meditation and obedience are important follow-up steps, although God may not reveal His *entire* plan at one time.

The second series of questions she honestly asks herself are, "What do I enjoy doing?" "What are my gifts?" "What would I do if time, space, and resources were not issues?" "What would I do if it did not matter what other people thought about what I did?" "What am I good at?" What is the use in living in a dream house if we do not live out our dreams? God has a great mission and plan for your life, and until you seek Him for it, you could spend your entire life working to pay bills and doing just enough not to lose a job. You will be caught in a press of busyness or what one of my mentor's Cecelia Williams Bryant calls "overbusyness" while bearing little or no good fruit.

As an undergraduate English major, I became fascinated with Nathanial Hawthorne's works because he was a free spirit, seemingly guided by his own God-consciousness. When he was a young man, Nathanial Hawthorne wrote, "I do not want to be a doctor and live by men's diseases, nor a minister and live by their sins, nor a lawyer and live by their quarrels. So , I don't see that there is anything left for me but to be an author." Our choices are not as limited as Hawthorne's were in his day. But we do get the point of his discourse. Seek and find, then act.

PROBLEMS IN THE FLOOR PLAN
(WON'T LET NOTHIN' TURN ME 'ROUND)

A woman at peace and joy has a focus and a fresh per-spective on adversity, so that nothing can turn her around. Once God gives you your purpose, call or ministry, you will see adversity. The Bible teaches that the devil came to "kill, steal, and destroy..." But don't let the problems in the floor plan of your dream house steal your joy, deter you, or rob you of your highest good.

A Fresh Perspective On Adversity

A woman at peace and joy needs a fresh perspective on adversity so that trials do not distract her from her destiny. Jesus said in John 16:33, "In this world you will have trouble, but take heart because I have overcome the world." Princesses take heart during times of adversity because we know that Jesus has overcome the cross and the entire world; therefore, whatever season we find ourselves in, it too, shall come to pass. That is great news!

The analogy of a home has is helpful in helping us to examine our perspectives in hopes of living like princesses in dream houses, but many in our global community are homeless. Some are homeless as a result of hurricanes, earthquakes, floods, medical issues including mental illness, substance abuse, and unemployment. I pray God's best and benediction upon them. At the same time, I thank God and a whole lot of angels, that I have always had a roof over my head, a warm bed, electricity, telephone services, and good food to eat.

I have never experienced homelessness, but I have experienced adversity. Your rock or hard place may not be physical homelessness or facing eviction, but if you have lived long enough, you will see adversity. But let's call James. What did James say? "Consider it pure joy, my brothers, whenever you face trials of many kinds, because you know that the testing of your faith develops perseverance. Perseverance must finish its work so that you may be mature and complete, not lacking anything. If any of you lacks wisdom, he should ask God, who gives generously to all without finding fault, and it will be given to him. But when he asks, he must believe and not doubt, because he who doubts is like a wave of the sea, blown and tossed by the wind" (James 1: 2-8).

The pressed are blown and tossed by the wind. Princesses, face adversity, live through it, grow stronger and deeper through it, and come out not lacking anything. She comes out as an Ntozake princess. Ntozake means, "she who brings her own things." She brings her own things to a table set by a King in a dream house. After all, what good is a nice house if nobody is home? Princesses come home to wisdom through adversity and when we look back at the illness prior to surgery, job termination, death of a loved one, death of a relationship, or season of poverty, we consider it as pure joy. Pure joy! I am really feeling this. Can you feel this? God is so amazing.

I am reminded of a televised sermon I heard one of my favorite Bible teachers, Charles Stanley, preach in 1997 on the subject of adversity. He taught me three things.

First, adversity makes us closer to and more dependent on God. When we come through the "homeless season," we can say like the Psalmist, "It was good for me to be afflicted so that I might learn your decrees." (Psalm 119:71) Princesses can honesty value affliction because through the affliction we become wiser and we sincerely value the wisdom contained in God's laws since "the law from [God's] mouth is more precious to [us] than thousands of pieces of silver and gold" (Psalm 119:72).

Second, princesses view adversity as coming *from* God, then there is no bitterness. I believe that God does not cause all situations which we view as adverse, but that He may permit them. Princesses cannot become or stay bitter with a loving heavenly Father.

Third, princesses ask, "What is it God wants to teach me through this season?" rather than focusing on what others may perceive as negative.

Finally, the princess sits on her throne in her dream house confidently after coming through (or while going through) an adverse situation because *she trusts God*. Her hope is built on nothing less than Jesus' blood and righteousness. She says like the Psalmist, "some trust in chariots, some in horses, but [I] trust in the name of the Lord our God" (Psalm 20:7). If Jesus had not trusted God, there would have been no Calvary and no blood to cover our many sins. There would be no dreams and no dream houses. There would be no princesses and there would be no pressed. There would be no me, and there would be no you.

"Is God Punishing Me?"

There will be problems when we are determined to live in peace and joy and live out our destinies. If we have conviction and faith we can run this race and know that God is not punishing us; rather he is grooming us and developing a special brand of wisdom within us that is a rare asset to all princesses who wish to remain on their thrones.

We will see trouble, adversity and minor inconveniences, but they can not throw us off the dream-land, princess track. Major tragedies and minor inconveniences come our way. The death of a child, parent or beloved spouse; the terminal illness of a parent; the loss of physical or mental abilities; are all major tragedies in this life, but the princess makes it through because she can distinguish between what Michael Kelly calls "the real" and "the role." Princesses understand that the real of us, which according to Genesis, is created in the image of God. We cannot add or detract from the real, because as God's image, the real is perfect, complete, and stable. On the other hand, the roles of mother, wife, teacher, daughter, aunt, cousin, friend, are those things which end once life on this earth is over. The real is eternal and lives forever; and embracing this, the princess can face major tragedies and still trust, and still plan, and still dream, and still prosper. Since princesses embrace the real and are divinely connected to the Eternal God, we are not derailed by what would literally kill some pressed women.

In contrast to major tragedies, we all face minor inconveniences. I am reminded of a minor inconvenience, as I see it: When I first saw the Sea Farer, I wanted it. The other homes, some newer, some bigger, which I saw afterwards paled in comparison, because it was my literal dream house in a dream location.

Our friend and real estate agent, Ann Bethel, will testify that I did not even want to get out of her car to see other homes after I had seen the Sea Farer. But when El Ninos aftermath came through this Virginia town of about 55,000 families and I saw my next door neighbors river meet them at the back door, I was more prayerful but not shaken. I thanked God for keeping us safe in what was called the worst storm on the Virginia Peninsula since the 1960s. My school notebooks and some priceless home videos were ruined, but I did not wish, for one minute that I did not live there at that time. I got the raft and some other beach toys, and we made lemonade out of lemons.

Everything we are going through will come to pass. "The joy of the Lord is my strength" not the joy of my ability to win battles because as that great political philosopher, Yogi

Berra, said, "it ain't over 'til its over." When it is over we realize that the battles all belong to God, not to us. We can't figure it all out, but we serve a God who has created it all and has figured it all out. God knew at the foundation of the world every situation we would face and what the outcomes would be. If we want to have freedom in our dream homes, we need to believe God to help us live out our destinies in spite of and in some cases, because of, adversity. As the old saints would say, "we have got to learn from our burns," which makes us wiser and more able to handle the next "giant." For as we see in the life of King David, giants keep coming. He slew Goliath as a boy, but that was not the last "giant" he had to confront in his earthly life.

Staying on the dreamland track in terms of fulfilling our destiny requires a deep trust in God in spite of adversity. In addition, we need prayers which go up like incense, and planning. I can say, as a princess who spent eleven consecutive years as a college honor student, that prayer and planning have a lot more to do with my academic and co-curricular success than does intelligence. We can't measure intelligence like we measure water. Each of us, I believe has different intelligences. Just because Trina is a superstar physicist does not make her any more or less intelligent than Kim who is the most gifted, female surgeon in her field, in the world, or any more or less intelligent that Jan who runs a bright and beautiful flower shop in Harvard Square.

TIME TO ARRANGE THINGS
(THE BLUEPRINT FOR PLANNING MY PERSONAL LIFE)

A woman at peace plans for her personal life which includes spiritual development, family life and finances.

The Psalmist tells us in Psalm 145:9 that God's understanding has no limit. We need to pray more than we plan, trust God more than we plan, but we need to plan. Kingdom women ought to have a plan for every area of life.

A DAILY APPOINTMENT WITH GOD

Princesses wake each day and ask the Master Architect for her marching orders. She spends uninterrupted time with the Father committing her day to Him and listening to Him. She makes her daily appointment with him more important than anything else. On the other hand, the pressed spend more time taking care of the whole world, and rush to spend time with God when they are in the car or the shower or when they run into a brick wall. As a princess, I have learned that silence and prayer are my best friends. The more time I spend with God, the more dreamlike my life is like, for the prophet Isaiah prophesied: "I know the plans I have for you, plans to prosper you, not to harm you, plans to give you hope and a future" (Isaiah 29:11).

One of my personal goals is to memorize as much Word as I can because the Apostle Paul teaches that, "the weapons we fight with are not the weapons of the world. On the contrary, they have divine power to demolish strongholds. We demolish arguments and every pretension that sets itself up against the knowledge of God, and we take captive every thought to make it obedient to Christ. ...You are looking only on the surface of things." (2 Corinthians 10:4-7). The pressed only look on the surface of things, but princesses know that there is a war going on and the enemy wants to steal peace and joy. Princesses mediate on God's word day and night and are careful to do everything written in it, so that her way is prosperous and successful. I don't know about you, but I am prosperous and successful, based on what God speaks into my life, not based on OPO (Other People's Opinions); therefore I live and move in the things dreams are made of; and I am deeply grateful to my Father in heaven.

FRUITFUL FAMILY LIFE IN THE HOUSE FIT FOR A PRINCESS

Princesses prioritize: God first, family second, and everything else third. She has a blueprint for a fruitful family life.

Scripture teaches that, "He who finds a good wife finds a good thing"; therefore, princesses do not *look* for husbands, but when and if God plans for them to marry, they spend more time in prayer and God-centered premarital counseling than they choosing a gown, invitations, china, menu, and reception hall. In the first three chapters of Genesis, everything God created was "good"; but when he created man and woman, God said it was "very good." The only thing that was not good was for man to be alone (Genesis 2:18).

THE STEWARDSHIP OF SEXUALITY

Although sex, I believe, is a gift God gives to married people, I was not a cloistered nun or virgin when I married. I thank God for his graciousness to me. I have learned, however, that God has given us stewardship over our own sexuality. When Jesus died for us, He shed his blood— it was a blood covenant. When a husband and his virgin wife consummate their marriage in the sex act, her hymen is broken, and her blood covers his penis. This too, is a blood covenant. Yes, sex and foreplay feel good, but princesses do not operate out of feeling alone. When you are intimate with someone, you give them a part of yourself. In addition, sexually transmitted disease can be spread, hearts can be broken, and unplanned pregnancies can occur.

Having a child is definitely a beautiful experience, *but it's really special when the child come at the right time in your life.*

Princesses are good stewards over their sexuality. They plan, with their husbands for the right time to conceive and give birth to the next generation. Tiger was conceived in London or Egypt while Myron and I were on a pilgrimage to the Holy Land where be baptized each other in the Jordan River. We were married six years before he was conceived, because we had a plan. Princesses value the marital relationship and plan for the next generation.

THE MINISTRY OF MOTHERHOOD

In the context of planning, Kingdom women ought to pray about how much pre-baby bonding they need with their husband, the head of her home. No matter how saved he is, it is work starting a family. Motherhood is a ministry, but it comes second to the ministry of marriage. Paul told the church at Ephesus that a husband should love his wife and be willing to lay down his very life for her, (not for his children). He goes on to say that the wife should submit to her husband as unto the Lord. You say, "Judi, you are taking us back twenty years." But in truth, any body with more than one head is abnormal and should be in a circus, not a dream house, and when the husband is one hundred percent loving, the wife is one hundred percent submitting.

The Bible teaches us that we are born sinful, but children come here full of love and light, ready to be trained up in the way in which they should go. They don't come here hostile. We make them that way when we neglect them, work out adult problems in their presence, treat them like little adults rather than children, fail to listen, fail to read to them. We make them that way when we don't have a prayer or a plan; and no matter how dream like the house is, the children can turn it into a nightmare if they are not disciplined, trained, loved and valued.

If you think day cares are warehouses, have a plan. The single family dream house may have to wait so you can live off of one income. If you plan to breastfeed, have a prayer and a plan. You can pump milk, but it is difficult to integrate the bonding factor if you are on the subway and your beloved child is home with the nanny. As a nudist, I thank God for my body, and I appreciate it. If you look nice in your bathing suit or birthday suit, Hallelujah; but I believe God gave us milk ducts and breasts to feed our babies. Baby cows drink cows milk. Baby humans drink breast milk. If you are not blessed to be able to let milk down, some cities even have milk banks. Have a plan and a prayer. The baby may have to wait until graduate school is almost over, because if your child has a fever and you have an exam, where are you going to be? At home at the cradle.

A common saying is, "she who rocks the cradle rules the world." I think God rules the world, but you get the point. God has gifted mothers to be in a position to train up children the Bible way, to create consciences, and to hone the fruits of the Spirit, to steward and touch the next generation. We plan to make our nail appointments, we plan how we are going to pay our car payments and taxes, we plan $30,000 weddings on ten dollar budgets, but motherhood is the most important work we will ever do, because in many ways we reproduce ourselves. Every princess ought to have a prayer and a plan for motherhood.

Paying The Mortgage

No matter how much or how little money we have, we cannot walk in true peace and joy until we have a plan for it. No, the color of peace is not green, as we discussed earlier. No, we are not of the world, but we live in a capitalistic world where we ought to have a plan for our finances. Every princess ought to invest her money wisely. Unless we find it, win it, inherit it, or steal it, one way to accumulate wealth or prepare for the future is to invest it wisely. It is wise to pray about investments, but one secure method is to place your money in a mutual fund, which is managed by a professional money manager (who will lose her or his job if they do not perform well for you). I have found that there are also advantages to investing in bond index funds which are simple because by choosing one fund, you gain exposure to either a specific segment of the United States bond market or the entire market. It also offers investors broad diversification.

Financially, successful princesses have financially successful mentors and coaches teachers. I was taught to go to school, earn good grades, go to college and graduate school and get a good job and earn money. Many of us were taught from this school of thought. However, I have seen so many who did all of these things, work for thirty years, retire, get a watch or a clock, and then cannot even afford to pay for their burial services. I have found that it is good to have a coach or teacher who is financially successful and learn from him or her.

Let's face it, we need financial freedom to impact this generation. To open and run battered women's shelters, programs for children and the elderly, we need money. And when we have wealth, we do not need a congressional act in order to be about our Father's business—we simply do it. We do not have to have city council's approval for a feeding program for the homeless; we simply rent a facility, open it and feed them! It is just that simple. In addition, princesses need financial freedom in order to have the flexibility to wear the many hats we are called to wear. God gives us direction in our finances for He owns and created it all.

FOCUSING ON THE FLOOR PLAN

Although princesses focus primarily on God in order to live in peace and joy, we ought to focus on our destinies in order to fulfill our dreams and the plans God has for each of our lives. I am not alone in recognizing the importance of setting firm priorities. As I interviewed women for this book, a common theme among the 274 women in my study was that they feel torn in many different directions. They feel as if they have to "juggle" just to make it each day. Ironing a blouse or writing checks, the routine things of daily life, coupled with the not-so-routine episodes like replacing your transmission or planning a funeral or moving, take up so much energy. Although some things are necessary, everything is not.

Lanna, a thirty six-year-old hairstylist, told me that the number one trap for her is "distraction." She said, "the devil tries to distract me from where God wants me to be... keeping me so busy doing everything else but what God told me to do." Fifty-two-year-old Vanessa said, "I go in so many directions that I am not good at anything. I stay up late cleaning, work all day, so the time I have with my family is not good because I'm irritable and have a bad attitude."

It is true, when we are sleep-deprived, we are more irritable and more likely to be clumsy. The front door of our lives becomes beat up from neglect within the house, while the devil tries to rob our rest, creativity, and time. There is always a trash can to clean or a cob web to dismantle, but what is really important? Who cares if your shirt is wrinkled, anyway? You are worthwhile because you belong to God, not because your house is clean or because of you run three miles each morning. The gift of eternal life is not based on the good things you do; it is based on the sacrifice Jesus made when He died at Calvary. In other words, you don't work your way into heaven or "good deed" your way into eternal fellowship with Him. Eternal life is a free gift.

We need simply to ask God for the strength to do what He has gifted us to do at each season of our lives. If we try to do everything that is "good" or everything that others are doing, we will not have time for our specific mission and purpose. God wants to give each of us discernment and help us focus on His specific will for our lives. Each morning I pray, "Father I commit this day to you." Why? Because He's also given us specific things to do each day, as well as in each season.

So we need to examine our priorities as we focus on the call on our lives. I'm not taking care of Tiger's hair or skin because I don't want people to say, "Hmm. Look at that ashy child." I do those things because I love him.

Princesses don't work to have the best yard on the block to impress others, but so they can show God they appreciate His gifts and they are good stewards who are faithful over a few things. Have you ever noticed how some kids starting out want their own apartment but they can't even keep their own rooms clean? Or how someone wants her own home but she can't even pay her rent on time? Remember how in the parable of the talents, Jesus says in Matthew 25:23, "You have been faithful over a few things, I will make thee ruler over many things." In other words, God has the whole world at His fingers and He'll bless you with what you need when He knows your motives and your heart are faithful and right.

That means determining what, and why, we should do certain tasks each day. Everything that is good to do, say in a 24-hour-period, is not always the best for you to do. Sure, you can weed the flower boxes on the front porch. I know it would look nice. But we are not in this race to see who has the prettiest flowers, or the most tastefully decorated yard, or the nicest car in the driveway. We are in this race to win people for Christ, to spread love, and to accomplish the specific missions God designed each of us to complete at the foundation of the world.

As we re-examine our priorities and how they relate to the design God has for our lives, we need to be aware that the devil sometimes uses "good things" to consume our time and energy to keep us from fulfilling the *best* things, which are those God has specifically called us to do. We can never steal a moment or a day back. Once the day is over, it is over.

While working on the first draft of this chapter, the mailman came, my father dropped by to see Tiger while he was napping, I prayed with a bereaved friend in Colorado over the phone, prayed with a long-time friend and her husband, made some arrangements for a baby shower, made a salad, fed the rabbits, and flossed my teeth—all within a three-hour time span. Even now, I could be steaming squash, washing clothes, washing my hair, giving my grandmother a bath in Williamsburg, planning our son's birthday party, planning my sister's surprise going-away party, or visiting my parents. They are all great things to do. But since I have the time and the Anointing to write—I'm writing. That is what God has called me to do during this season in my life. I do not have a single focus, but if I never do it, it will never get done. Right now, I don't have time to juggle. I am trying to reach you, teach you and encourage you (and grow deeper internally)—even as I simmer beans and rice and listen for my napping son and three godchildren. This is life.

I am reminded of a cartoon photocopy quantitative research professor and a faithful member of my dissertation committee, Barbara Neufeld, shared with me. The cartoon shows a woman writing. After each frame with her writing, she was depicted doing something completely different: Frame One: woman writes. Frame Two: woman vacuums. Frame Three: woman writes. Frame Four: woman cleans bathroom. Frame Five: woman writes. Frame Six: woman waters plants. Frame Seven: woman writes. Frame Eight: woman cleans windows. You get the idea.

There are a million and one reasons to keep us from our purposefully productive frame and trap us in a meaningless frame. Don't get me wrong. Windows have to be washed—I guess. Plants have to be watered, but everything in its own time. Don't juggle. Prioritize according to the goals God has given you and focus. As we do, our homes and lives will be peaceful and calm, and inviting to others to come in and partake of the serenity.

But how do we get there? The following principles form the word "FOCUS"; they will help ground you in your purpose so that you will be less likely to wither before you begin to blossom. In the process, your inner beauty will develop and create an outward glow that's contagious. Expect no less, for you *are* a princess.

F is for faith. Every princess ought to have faith in God and faith in herself. Faith is part in our hearts and part in our mouths. It is part what we believe and part what we confess. We need faith in our hearts about what we can't see and faith in our mouths about what we say. Jesus said that if we have faith even as small as a mustard seed, that we can say to the mountain, "be moved" and it will move from here to there (Matthew 17: 20, 21). I don't know about you sister friends, but I believe God for and dream about: mountain moving, net breaking, boat sinking, devil stomping, take no prisoners, say what you will, childlike, don't care what the world thinks, mustard seed faith.

In two of the Synoptic Gospels, Mark and Matthew, the writers record a story of the healing of a demon-possessed boy. The boy's father pleaded for help. I was not there, but using my sanctified imagination, I can just imagine that they took the boy to the church, and they could not do a thing to help him. They took him to the river and could not do a thing. They took him to the women's Bible study luncheon, and they could not do a thing. They took the boy to Jesus' disciples and they could not help him either. Jesus said, "you faithless and perverse generation." He then asked, "How long must I be with you? How long must I do these things for you?" Finally, the boy's father went to Jesus and said, "*if* you can" heal him, please do so. Jesus, questioning the father's faith asked, "*if* I can?" And He healed the boy. Jesus' disciples asked, "why couldn't *we* do it?" "Why couldn't we drive that demon out?" Jesus replied, "this kind can only come by prayer" (Matthew 17:22). The spiritual application here is that a strong prayer life helps to cultivate the faith we need to fulfill our purposes and live in peace and joy. Jesus need not do these things for us; God has given us everything necessary to do even greater things, *if* we would only believe.

In addition to faith in God, we ought to have faith in ourselves since "we are God's workmanship, created in Christ Jesus to do good works which God prepared in advance for us to do" (Ephesians 3:20). I believe that no weapon formed against me shall proper, and I walk in my prosperity. I believe that I am more than a conqueror because of God's love; and I can trample over serpents without being harmed. I can't teach this thing into you because faith is personal. We have to speak it to ourselves. Cultivate it, walk in it, and it will cause you to focus on what is necessary to create heaven on earth.

O stands for "outside distractions." We discussed this as we decided earlier not to get caught up in every cob web we encounter. Princesses make conscious decisions not to get caught up in every distraction. Every thing that is good to do, I have learned, is not the best thing to do. At this moment, it is almost 6:00 am. I could be balancing my check-book, sorting Tiger's socks, making plans for my relocation, washing my hair, finishing the book, *Sayings of Paramanhansa Yogananda*, writing my Aunt Tiny in Los Angeles or my mother in Hampton, giving myself a pedicure, laying on the phone *talking* about my plans, or penning a few thank you cards. They are all good things to do, but God has given me this time, a fresh mind, and this silence in order to focus on this task so that I might be reminded that He has called me to touch this generation for Him. The Holy Spirit gives me the ability to discern between that which is necessary and that which is distraction. [As an aside, Tiger came into my study, crawled on my back, began stroking my hair and prayed: "God, please help mommy to get a good book out. {He is one of great helpers.} I hope her book goes out good and I will hope she receives her good. I hope her book goes out very good. In Jesus' name. Amen.] My boy is not a dis-traction. Rather, he is a blessing, an encouragement, a splash of sweetness in my life.

Princesses edit any activities or relationships that do not line up with God's purpose for our lives and subse-quent goals. Do not rely on our culture, your feelings or intellect; rely on your faith and the truth in God's Word. If a person or event or habit does not bring God glory or contribute to your mission—edit it.

C stands for "call." Princesses realize that we have spe-cial calls on our lives. Pam may be called to teach nutrition; Deborah is called to be a bright light in the field of human resources; while Quintina may be called to be liturgical dancer and evangelist. God has a great plan for and call on your life. Don't simply dream about it, walk in it.

U is for understanding. Princesses understand that each part of the Body of Christ has a different function. The light cannot say to the microphone, "because you do not brighten the room, there is no need for you." The light understands that it is her job to illuminate and it is the function of the microphone to magnify sound.

One of my favorite songs goes something like this, "what God has for me, it is for me. What God has for me, it is for me. [As Tiger sings along with me as he sits on my shoulders]. I know without a doubt, that He will work it out. What God has for me, it is for me." What God has for you is for you. Nobody can add to it or take away from it. This is why it is fruitless to compare, judge, and critique. Princesses simply flow in what is for them. Are you feeling this? Good.

S stands for sensitivity. As a princess, living in a dream house I have to be prayerful and sensitive to the millions of pressed women who walk around talking about how bad it is; comparing themselves to others; holding grudges; and who never advance in their purpose or the things of God. When princesses lose the sensitivity factor, they become cynical, self-righteous, distracted and pressed. The pressed looks at the homeless, incarcerated drug addict saying, "she came from a two-parent home, went to an Ivy League school, and never had to struggle, she *should* be working in corporate America. She *should* be taking care of her husband and children." The princess looks at the same woman and prays because everything she sees gives rise to prayer. She looks at the same women and thinks, "perhaps her spirit came here to become homeless, addicted and incarcerated to teach me and the rest of the world to be grateful for our stations." The princess is well aware that an incarcerated, addict could very well shine a brighter light than a Bishop in a church. She realizes it is not for her to judge the brightness of anyone's light nor is it her place to critique every one's situation for only God has all of the information.

We need to be sensitive to the millions of women and men who wander aimlessly, trying to impress others. They simply exist. Some people never know God intimately, never listen to Him; therefore, they may look well, seem well, and do well, but they will never reach their full, divine potential until they line up with God. Be sensitive to those who only look at the front door, who do not have the knowledge and understanding about God and His Law. Remember, we are all in the process of evolving. Pray for them! (And pray for me while you're at it!)

So princesses focus and listen. We listen to God and ask Him for his Anointing, His Power. We listen and, as Claudette Anderson Copeland puts it, "we find the spot where the oil comes out." The pressed look and say, "I want to look like Vanessa Williams, Anoint it." "I want to have a ministry like Joyce Meyers, Anoint it." "I want to sing like her, dress like her, and live in a dream house like her (when they have no idea what is behind the front door); Anoint what I need to get me there." That is crazy! The devil wants to drive you crazy, but he is the father of lies! Amen, belongs right there.

I have learned that God's Anointing only activates in Divine will. God did not say He would bless our mess. What did Paul tell the Romans in the eight chapter? This entire chapter is shouting ground, but Paul says," All things [not some things—all things] work together for good for those who love God and are called according to *His* purposes" (Romans 8:28). When we try to operate outside of the Anointing of God, we become miserable, depressed, pressed, suicidal—yes, because if the enemy had his way we would all be on the back ward of a mental ward wearing pink smocks swatting flies that are not even in the air. This is a strong emotional word picture, but mental illness is no joke. It is not funny. As a people of God, we need to pray about it, and believe God for healing in this area just as fervently as we pray about healing for physical maladies such as breast cancer, AIDS, hypertension, lupus, and heart disease. Half of the world is on medication to stabilize a mental or emotional imbalance.

Friends, don't follow the crowd. All of your sister friends may be ushers, you feel badly because you don't feel called to do that. God may have called you to help with their children or do their hair so that they can serve and look pretty at the same time. Princesses know that it is critical to focus, but without the Anointing and divine favor of God it is fruitless.

WHY AM I BEHIND THIS COMPUTER AT THIS TIME? (THE BLUEPRINT FOR PLANNING MY PROFESSIONAL LIFE)

A woman at peace and joy plans for her life's work and works to fashion a plan which takes into consideration her gifts, preferences, temperament, needed skills and the specific call on her life.

While teaching a religion course at Saint Leo College in Virginia and while doing a live television interview and call-in show for the Christian Television Network in Michigan, I realized that I was called to respond, on my feet, to the concerns of people as they relate to spiritual matters. No, I do not have all of the answers. If I do not know an answer to a question, I simply say, "I do not know." However, I enjoy it, and I am good at it. I have to plan my professional life based on what God has given me. I am in front of this computer monitor at this time, because I am planning for my professional life, my ministry. I am planning to touch this generation with books and conferences which help us all grow more like Christ. That is why I am here doing what I am doing. Why are you doing what you are doing? This is not a rhetorical question. Although we have examined the area of motives, it is critical to revisit here because why plan, if you are motivated to go into an area where there is no Anointing, no oil, no power, no desire, no gifts? Every princess has a plan for her professional life.

We ought to be flexible and teachable but we ought to plan. We give birth to babies and movements and ideas which is an awesome responsibility, but if we are to impact this generation with the things dreams are made of, we need to pray more than we plan, but we have got to plan.

If it is your professional dream to become a consultant at McKenzie and earn $300,000 plus bonuses annually, you need a plan. You ought to find out what it took others to get there, and plan your life accordingly or you will be caught in the press. If you need to earn an Masters of Business Administration and travel internationally, you need to plan. Where do the children come in? Is motherhood part of the plan? Are healthy dinners and quiet time part of the plan? I am not running this down to discourage you. We need princesses in corporate America, but if you earn $300,000 each year, believe me. You will earn it.

God revealed to me that my ministry would cross racial lines, so I had to plan to get the credentials which I appreciate, but which I needed to have in order to get all races to at least listen. Whether I am in the white house or a drug detox house, people know Harvard. Although we are not of the world, we live in the world; and God allows us to plan to obtain all that is necessary to do his work in the world. A close friend once said, "if I had the parents you have, I would have gone to Harvard, too." I have four siblings. At this point, I am the only Harvard graduate. It is not about Harvard; rather it is about God giving me what was necessary to do what he sent me to earth to do. Princesses plan. Princesses can't be on the wrong road and end up in the right place. Plan.

I was not born with four degrees, driving a Mercedes, and traveling the world teaching. God has been gracious to me, but I had to have a plan. While a high school student, I worked as a bus girl, dishwasher, and expediter at a tavern in Virginia. I saw folks with three children doing what I was doing to pay rent. I saw the way some of the managers talked to and put their hands on the employees. I began praying and planning and getting serious. I planned to go to college. And I planned to make straight "As" (although I earned three or four "Bs" as an undergraduate)— not because grades measure anything, but because I knew I needed good letter grades to get into Harvard or any other good graduate school. I planned to get involved co-curricularly, because my father, a retired university dean, would often say, "of course you can make good grades if that is all you do." So I had a planned to get involved in student government and volunteerism. Everything did not turn out like I had planned, but I did not get caught in the press because I had a plan, a dream. Ask yourself the following series of questions if you are still constructing your professional plan, and dream while you are pondering the answers.

Questions To Consider:

1. Where do I work best (home, home/office, office building, outside, alone, in a group, where I have to be more cerebral or more creative)?

2. Do I need a formal education to fulfill my destiny? Not sure? Get one anyway and keep listening to God. It does not matter your age, resources or ability. God will make up the difference.

Consider volunteering, or serving as an intern to find out what others in your field actually do all day and whether you feel called to do it; but whatever you do, have a plan and follow the Master Architect.

Princesses do what they can with what they have and the pressed mourn over what they do not have. We need to do what we have the grace and gifts to do, what we are called to do.

Use It Or Lose It

A woman at peace and joy knows that if she does not exercise her gifts and operate in the grace given her, she may lose the gift and the grace. As in the Matthean parable of the talents, God entrusts each of us with certain gifts according to our level of ability. No matter what God entrusts us with, He expects us to increase it, use it. A princess uses her gifts and multiplies her talents and light in the world and is given much more. The pressed, on the other hand, hide their talents because of fear and lack of faith; and consequently they are taken from them (Matthew 25: 16-18). Princesses know that we have to use what God has given us or we could lose it.

Awnings rot, windows get stuck, pipes and tanks rust— when we don't use them, and so it is with our talents. I am reminded of a childhood friend who held her hand over her heart after her beloved mother died. Today she is a grown woman with a small, disfigured arm. Since she never used her arm, its growth was stunted. Perhaps her spirit came to give us each an emotional picture of what literally happens when we do not use what our loving heavenly Father has graced us with.

CHAPTER TEN

Ordering My Steps In The Things Dreams Are Made Of

Principle: In order to live in peace, I must accept the fact that I am in need of self-examination.

Confession: It is time for me to walk in the peace that is rightfully mine, today!

A woman at peace and joy knows that she must accept the fact that we are all in need of self examination. More importantly, we need to meditate on what God says to us. He speaks to His children daily; and for me it is my life's single greatest privilege.

Christ has left his peace with us according to John 14:27, but it seems so elusive because we live in the flesh, and we only see today, our current circumstances, and the problems and demands of our tiny worlds. In the flesh, we try to figure things out, but God says to us, "while you are trying to figure it out, I have already worked it out." We need more faith so that we can walk in the gift of peace. Hebrews 11:1 says, "Faith is being sure of what we hope for, and certain of what we do not see."

I am currently going through a divorce, dealing with issues such as the "death" of a relationship, the end of a season of my life, custody issues, property settlements, taxes, but I thank God that I am at peace—I have a song on my heart. Like the Psalmist, I don't need a choir or an orchestra, because, "over my head, I hear music in the air." Don't get me wrong, sister friends, I cry sometimes. Sometimes, I cry a little, then pray a little, pray in the spirit, pray in English, cry and pray, but I have a peace and joy that this world does not understand because although I do not *see* how things are going to work out, although I do not *see* why some folks value the things which they value in this situation, although I do not *see* what my life will be like in six months or six years or six days, I am sure of what I hope for. I am sure that nothing can separate me from the love of God. I am sure that I will not have unforgiveness and self condemnation holding me from God's highest good for my life. I am sure that this peace I have, the world didn't give it to me, and the world can't take it away. When we are limited in faith, we limit our peace. When we expand our faith, we walk in peace.

Peace is a gift. Ollie and I have several gifts under the Christmas tree which we plan to open on Christmas morning. The one from his Aunt Margaret-Ann is even marked, "do not open until Christmas." If we do not open them, then we will never know what is inside. Imagine receiving a beautifully wrapped gift and *never* opening it. Peace is a beautiful gift which must be opened because we cannot passively receive it. We must actively claim it in order to walk in it.

We have to want to open the gift of peace. We have to desire a life of peace before we can have it. Have you ever heard of the sayings, "You'll have what you say," or "You'll see what you say"? We must want to see peace in order to actually see it, live it, walk in it. I am reminded of the story John tells in Chapter five, verses one through eight. Walter Thomas' sermon from this pericope, "Rise, Pick Up Your Mat, and Walk!," has inspired me to use it as an illustration for seeking peace.

Many of us want peace but much of what we face we have little idea what to do about. John has a very significant word for us. His story shows us one person's pain. Forget his gender for a moment, that is not important. John does not even tell us the man's name because he represents any and every pressed person. He represents someone seeking peace. It does not matter who you are, where you come from or your pedigree, sometimes a spirit of heaviness, a spirit from hell will hang over you. But the Word of God teaches us that God has given us dominion over our problems and "peacelessness" and all of the works of the enemy. We have them under our feet. In John's story, we are not even certain of this man's ailment so we don't assume that the problem is only specific to him. Similarly, you are not the only one who needs peace. You are not the only one in the situation you are in—there are other women who were molested as a child. There are other women whose families of origin have forsaken them. There are other women who are in relationships that are too good to leave, but too bad to stay. There are other women who want a child but have never been able to conceive. There are other women who wake each morning wanting a drink or a pill or a snort more than they want their next breath. There are other women in nursing homes on feeding tubes hoping that they will not lose custody of their minor children because of their inability to physically care for them. There are other women who have to decide whether or not to pull the plug on the respirator in the neonatal intensive care unit. Like the man in John's story, our problems are not specific, but they are generalizable. They hurt us, but they have hurt others before. They hinder us, but they have hindered others.

All we know is that the man in John's story is an invalid. Walter Thomas says, that perhaps John left out the man's specific ailment so we don't assume that the problem is only specific to him. Fill your problem in that blank that John left for this man's ailment. The man had been sick for thirty eight years. Some of us have been looking for a life of peace for thirty eight years. Some of us have been allowing peace to allude us for years and years. So John tells us that this ailing man had been hanging with a bunch of other ailing people. I was not there, but the way John wrote the fifth chapter and the way Walter Thomas painted his picture, I can use my sanctified imagination and see this man hanging with others who had problems. I can imagine that they people were lying around the pool, perhaps calling the psychic hotline, perhaps just talking about their problems, talking about each other.

I have come to know in my young life that those who do not have peace—and it is possible to have an ailment and still have peace—seem to want to dwell on the misfortunes of themselves and others. Those who allow peace to allude them spend so much time worrying about who is fatter, more miserable, poorer, dumber, and uglier than they are. When we seek peace, it does us no good to hang with a bunch of folk who don't have it. Their spirits of hopelessness and complaining will rub off on us.

John tells us that one day, Jesus comes by. He knows just when to stop by. He knows that we need to know sorrow in order to appreciate joy. Jesus knows that in order to have mountain top experiences, we have to have gutter experiences. Jesus saw all of the sick people. He looked at the one man and asked, "Do you want to get well?" Jesus knows everything; and God knows our words before we even speak. Jesus asked the question, not to gain information, but to stimulate the man's thinking. "Do you want to get well?" I don't know about you, but I would have jumped and shouted, "Yes, Master, Yes!" But he did not answer Jesus' questions. Rather, he answered the question, "Why are you in this shape?" Thomas suggests that the man answered the unspoken question because that is the question we have lodged in our minds.

Like the man at the pool in John, we often deny ourselves peace because we are not concerned with the fact that peace is a gift from Jesus, rather we are concerned with the self-pitying question, "Why me?" When you have a pity party, the only ones present are you and the devil, God's enemy. So, then the question becomes for us, "Do we *want* to have peace?" Do we want to live as princesses in dream homes? Do we want to walk in peace? A whole lot of us are asking ourselves, "Why am I in this predicament?" Sometimes we have had strife in our lives for so long that it is all we talk about. Your husband walked out on you twenty years ago, and you can't minister to anyone because when they need God to speak to them through you, all you can talk about is that man who walked out and how he has not supported your children. Peace is yours because God supplies all of our needs according to *His* riches in glory in Christ Jesus, not because of what we can figure out or talk ourselves through.

No matter how long you have been depressed, peace is a gift, but you must open it!

No matter how long you have been trying to fulfill your purpose in life, peace is a gift, but you must open it!

No matter how long you have been ill, peace is a gift, but you must open it!

No matter how long you have been staring consumer debt and student loans in the face, peace is a gift, but you must open it!

You may think it is impossible to love yourself, your body, your temperament, your gifts.

You may not be able to see yourself as stable, durable, healed, whole, and long-lived, incorruptible, but if you are certain that peace is your gift, you will make it.

The devil wants you to be overwhelmed by your circumstances. He wants you to run around like an ant building an ant house, trying to solve all of the problems of this world, but open the gift, and peace is yours.

You are in love with God. You have dedicated your life to Jesus. You attend church every Sunday; and you think you can handle anything. But there are spiritual battles, and problems in our lives that we have to turn over to God if we are to walk in the peace which belongs to us as princesses, heirs of the most high God.

There is a sister slumped over in her recliner, worrying about why her mother has never been there for her in ways which would minister to her need for mother love.

There is a sister who has been in bed for nine days who can't get up because her child died last month and nobody knows why.

There is a sister whose husband has a mental illness and she and her children live in fear and ride on a roller coaster. She loves him, but she is scared to death.

There is a sister who has had to act like a man, leave her children for strangers to rear, be aggressive when she prefers being polite, and eat high-fat, high-sodium food because she thinks her worth is connected to her salary.

There is a sister who has had her face in a pillow for ten years because she aborted a child as a teen; and as an adult she is physically barren.

There is a sister who, by the grace of God, missed a terrible car accident today, by one second because she was not thinking about driving, she was thinking, "why do my neighbors talk about me so much, when I try to be a good person?"

I have been there. Sometimes I lay in bed and moan, and say, "Daddy, hold me." I know that even when your mother and father forsake you—when those dearest to you, are not there in a time of need, God is there. God cares. And, that alone gives me peace.

The entire gospel of John teaches us that what we can't do, God and his warring angels can do. God has all power and all peace in the palm of his hand; and it is ours to claim, if we claim it in Jesus' name.

Jesus did not argue with the man at the pool. God has a standard; He will not come down to the pity pool where we are, He will bring us up to His standard. Jesus, said to the man, "Rise, pick up your mat, and walk!" Jesus says to us, "Rise, pick up your mat, and walk in peace."

The first step to opening the gift of peace is getting out of a state of darkness, confusion and defeat. Say to yourself, "I'm not looking back." "I'm standing on the promises of God." "I am going to rise!"

Get up. Rise. Stop talking about how horrible things are. Reframe. Rise. Stop worrying what someone else did or said. Rise. Stop trying to figure it out. Rise. Stop crying. Rise. Stop talking about others in order to minimize your pain. Rise! Jesus says, you have hungered and thirsted after righteousness long enough. Rise and be filled. Whatever you do, sister friends, rise! We have to get ourselves together, love ourselves, and believe that we deserve a life of peace and joy.

Your mother died during your birth, rise!

Your husband died when your oldest child was seven, rise!

You almost lost your mind earning your JD or MBA, rise!

Folks have lied on you at work, rise!

Your husband was good to you, but you committed adultery. God has forgiven you, rise!

Get up from that.

You charged someone with sexual harassment and no one believed you—God knows—rise!

Pregnant and no plans for marriage—rise!

Your oldest daughter verbally abuses you—rise!

Your husband beat you like a man, and now it's your fault—rise!

You lost your hair and eyebrows during chemotherapy—rise.

You are more than what you look like. You are more than what you and your children accomplish. You are more than your relationships. You are created in the image of the most high God. Rise!

The second step in opening the gift of peace is picking up our mats. Our mats, as Walter Thomas creatively describes it, are our problems. "Put them under your arm instead of under your life," he says. The mat is a symbol of our misery. Carry it. Many times we minister out of our brokenness. Our problems are a part of who we are. They make us stronger, wiser, more resilient and more aware of our need for God's power. So we do not discard them, we carry them. But at the same time we cannot let the people and problems in our lives overwhelm us and paralyze us. Put your mat in your brief case and carry it. You know it is there, but you carry it, it does not carry you. Those who do not walk in peace lay on the mat, those who do, carry it.

Open your gift of peace by putting your mat in your case.

Put being used in your case.

Put being neglected in your case.

Put waking every morning to a habit that is justified by your own ego in your case.

Put what folks say about your children in your case.

How can we lift our heads if we are down on a mat? I will lift up mine eyes to the hills from whence comes my help. My help comes from the Lord, not from public opinion, income, my pedigree or address. My help comes from the Lord. My peace comes from the Lord.

The third step to opening the gift of peace is walking. You say of the invalid in John's story, "he can't walk, he's an invalid." Jesus says, "walk." Steps one and two the man could do alone, but he could not take step three without making a leap of faith. Walk! Believe that you can, and do it! We have come full circle back to the need to increase our faith in order to open the gift of peace. Regardless of your limitations, walk. If you fall, God and his angels will be there to help you, but walk. Walk with the Lord. Walk in faith. As you walk, think of the "Footprints" poem. God has been with you every step, whether you know it or not. Walk, my sisters, walk!

Now that you have opened your gift, please know that a peaceful, joyful life is not a trouble-free life. But living in peace is sort of like being made of Teflon rather than flesh. The flesh wants to be unforgiving, jealous, and vengeful. But Teflon is resilient and always the same. Teflon takes no prisoners! It bounces back and seems almost untouchable. Peace is having a calm, exercising a calm which is based in faith. Walking in peace gives us a calm that the world does not understand because we rely on God's knowledge, strength, and grace, not our own.

Christ's desire is for us to live in peace, "to have life and to have it more abundantly." God did not save us just to take us to heaven; He wants us to enjoy this life, to live in peace. If He saved us just to take us, we would go to heaven as soon as we accepted Christ. Christ desires for us to receive His gift of peace so that we can experience God's unconditional love and so that our effectiveness will not be hindered in the earth.

Jesus taught his disciples to pray saying, "Our Father....thy kingdom come, thy will be done, *on earth as it is in heaven...*" Jesus wants us to have as much peace here as there is in heaven. In heaven there is no sickness, no strife, no mourning, no grief, no sorrow. (I believe if it were God's will to physically heal every person, there would be no sick or dead believers). Although we live in the flesh, and emotions like anger, grief, and rage are natural, when we live abundantly, as if we were in heaven, we are able to cast all of that stuff onto God because He cares for us. We don't have to hold all of the negative things that pollute our perspectives and drain us making our energy insufficient for the important things in life.

When Jesus died on Cavalry's tree at Golgotha's hill and rose on the third day, he gave us the most tremendous gift of peace. We have peace that we are redeemed. We have peace that no matter what we have done or said, when we seek forgiveness, we are washed and set right with God. God does not keep a record of what we did in 1977, 1997 or what we will do in 2007. He loves us, and made the sacrifice of His beloved Son possible so that we can fumble and stumble (and princesses do make mistakes) and still look to a Savior who hung high on a cross for our forgiveness. We also have the example in Jesus who hung on the cross and prayed for his enemies: "Father forgive them, for they do not know what they are doing." Similarly, we can have peace and pray for the sister-in-law, who because of the way she feels about herself, treats you harshly. We can pray for the professor who thinks you have it easier than he had it so he is unfair to you. We can pray for the sibling or best friend who thinks you had it too easy because of your good looks when only God and a whole lot of angels really know what you had to endure. Most of all, we have a Father who loves us unconditionally. That alone gives me peace and great joy.

Allow me to introduce you to Rebecca, a woman who has struggled and succeeded at finding God's peace in her everyday life. Rebecca was married twice, has buried both husbands, and reared five children. Her parents died in an accident when she was two; and her maternal aunt reared her, but always seemed to favor her biological children. Rebecca's first husband was physically and verbally abusive. She left him when she was pregnant with her fifth child. She went on to earn a baccalaureate degree in science at a time when most black women could only do domestic work. She struggled. Today she says, "it was a struggle, but it was a happy struggle." Years after the divorce from her first husband, he would call her for advice as if he were one of her children. Proverbs 31, says, "her children arise and call her blessed, *her husband also praises her.*"

After marrying her second husband, she found that he and his brothers had mental illnesses which caused them to be condescending, neglectful, brutal and isolating. She tried to show her husband the love of Christ, treating him the way she would want to be treated, but deep inside she had no peace. She tried to hold on to her vows, "for better or for worse," but in her prayer closet, God spoke to her and said, "I don't want you to live like this, you are my precious daughter. You are a queen." She separated from her husband, but never divorced him. He died a lonely death, and the paramedics who found him said it looked as if he struggled for the door during his last moments. Rebecca cried at his funeral. Her grown daughter rebuked her saying, "I don't want to see another tear. You are free and you don't know it."

When Rebecca decided to separate from her husband she had to examine herself by looking beyond that moment, that day, and look into the future. Today, she can look back and laugh about how mean her husbands had been to her. She has a peace and joy that the world can't comprehend because if the devil had his way she would have lost her mind.

She realized that she had to claim the peace Christ had promised her because she needed to be happy and fruitful. She needed to walk in the promises of God, not in the torment which she felt in her marriages.

I do not advocate divorce or separation, I use Rebecca's story to illustrate the way God spoke to her to make a change in her life. She did not change until she examined herself, a key component of which was listening to God. He had to speak specifically to her. He did not speak audibly the way you hear most speak, but a still, small voice from within spoke and gave her direction. She is lonely sometimes, but God is her everything: husband, friend, father—divine companion.

God has a great plan for your life. He wants you to live in peace. He does not want you to compare yourself to

Rebecca, me, or any other person. He wants you to examine yourself. He wants *you* to walk in peace.

Now that we have examined ourselves and laid the foundation for redesigning the blueprints of our dream homes, let us continue to revisit those problem areas in the floor plan, those floors which need sanding, the pictures that need reframing, and those places where we need periodic deep cleaning. Although this book is about self examination, we will never know peace and joy if all we have on our minds is ourselves. Jesus says, "If anyone would come after me, he must deny himself and take up his cross and follow me. For whoever wants to save his life will lose it, but whoever loses his life for me and for the gospel will save it" (Mark 8:34, 35). Princesses deny themselves because they follow the Prince of Peace.

Now that you have a blueprint for your dream house, you are called to leave your home and go into the world. Go out into the world in peace, hold onto what is good. Strengthen the faint, support the weak, help the suffering; and return no person, evil for evil. "God has called us to live in peace" (I Corinthians 14:33). It is a gift from our Beloved Lord who said, "peace I leave with you."

It is a gift and part of our birthright as heirs of the Most High God. You deserve to enjoy peace and joy and to express it. Peace is a healer. It is yours.

As women, we often take better care of the whole world than we take of ourselves. We want to take care of, fix and change everything on the outside when everything we need is within us. Once we accepted Christ, the fruits of the spirit, including peace and joy, were given as a gift. Everything you need to live in a dream house is already inside of you. Michael Kelly, told me a story about a species of deer called the musk deer. The musk deer smells the sweetest smelling fragrance. She runs to the north, south, east, and west, searching for the source of the wonderful aroma. She runs all day and all night searching. Finally, she becomes so exhausted that she falls to the ground. Her head drops to her navel—and there it is! *The fragrance comes from her own navel.* The spiritual application here is that the pressed woman runs around trying to live someone else's dream, or trying to find a relationship to give her peace, or trying to earn enough money to have peace; and all the while, *everything she needs is inside of her.* Princesses spend time in the silence, praying and planning, and enjoying the aroma which comes from inside of her for she knows that all she needs, God has already placed inside of her. If you are running and looking and pressed and homeless. Come to the place where princesses live. Come to your dream house because peace is a healer. Joy leads to ascension. You deserve them both.

Go out into the world in peace and joy. Let your light shine in your own special way. Princesses of the world, live in peace, abide in joy! You deserve it. So be it.

PRINCIPLES AND CONFESSIONS

1. **Principle:** In order to live in peace and joy, I must connect with God, and be clear on my motives for designing and projecting my personal image. I must not let others' opinions of me hinder God's plan for my life.

    Confession: I bring God glory because I am more concerned about pleasing Him than I am about living up to others' expectations of me, winning friends and impressing people. My image reflects my true character. They both bring glory to God and show His love in the earth.

2. **Principle:** In order to live in peace and joy, my relationships must not be the basis of my existence, and they must show the love of God and reflect His design and perfect will, thus I choose to edify and encourage the people in my life.

    Confession: My relationships and conversations build others up and reflect the love of Christ. The bread of gossip, criticism, and judgment I do not eat.

3. **Principle:** In order to live in peace and joy, I must be disciplined to sustain myself physically (drink clean water, eat plenty of vegetables, protein, fruit, and get enough exercise and rest).

Confession: My body is the temple of God. I will eat healthy foods. I will not dig my grave with my teeth. I will exercise and rest. However, I realize that I will not live by bread alone but by every Word that proceeds from the mouth of God. I live on His word so when I turn down my plate and fast, I still have what is necessary to prosper. I value proper diet and nutrition, but I know that the main thing is keeping the main thing the main thing.

4. **Principle:** In order to live in peace and joy, I must put the past in perspective, line my prayers up according to it, and move on.

   Confession: Today is a new day. My past is behind me. I chose to live in peace and joy this day.

5. **Principle:** In order to live in peace and joy, I must simplify my life and edit habits, attitudes, relationships and *things* that clutter my life, weigh me down and cause me to be less fruitful than I was created to be.

   Confession: I choose today to eliminate and bring to no effect, all of the distractions that keep me from a life of peace and joy.

6. **Principle:** In order to live in peace and joy, I must place God first and my husband second to all other relationships and things.

   Confession: God is my first love. My marriage comes second to my devotion to God. All other calls on my life follow these.

7. **Principle:** In order to live in peace and joy, I must be good to myself, pamper myself, and praise my Creator at the same time.

   Confession: I know that charm is deceptive and beauty is fleeting. And although my beauty comes from reverently and worshipfully serving the Lord, I take care of myself. And while I pamper myself, I praise my Creator.

8. **Principle:** In order to live in peace and joy, I must ask God for and focus on a plan for my personal life and a plan for my professional life. I must have a vision for my life.

   Confession: I pray more than I plan, but I plan so that I might have peace and joy, fulfill my destiny and touch my generation.